Islamic Soldiers serving in the Waffen-SS

Perry Pierik

Islamic Soldiers serving in the Waffen-SS

Aspekt Publishers

Islamic Soldiers serving in the Waffen-SS

© Perry Pierik
© 2023 ASPEKT Publishers
Amersfoortsestraat 27, 3769 AD Soesterberg, Nederland
info@uitgeverijaspekt.nl - www.uitgeverijaspekt.nl

First Edition 2023

Cover design: Mark Heuveling
Inside: BeCo DTP-Productions
Translation: Emy van Gorkom

ISBN: 9789464629699
NUR: 680

All rights reserved. Not part of this publication may be reproduced, stored in a retrieval system or transmitted in any forms or by any means, electronic, mechanical, photocopying, or recording or otherwise, without the prior permission of the publisher. *Licence: CC BY-SA 3.0

Table of contents

Introduction 9

Neu Turkestan Division. 19

Osttruppen 21

Kleinkrieg and Kosakentum 25

Hitler: "We Will Never Create a 'Russian Army'" 29

Mayer-Mader and the Turkmen Troops 33

Professor Oberländer and the "Sonderverband Bergmann" 35

The Collaboration with the Crimean Tatars 39

National Identity, Liberation Armies, and the German Occupation Policy 45

Oberländer and the Conflict About the Murders in Taman 49

Propaganda - Caucasian Journalists in Dabendorf 61

Writings, Memos, and the 24 Theses of Oberländer 65

THE SS Steals Soldiers from Army 71

From Division to Corps 81

Mayer-Mader vs. Hermann, Goals and Ambitions Concerning the Osttruppen 85

Trouble in Polish Trawniki 95

Transfer to Minsk and Juraciszki 97

The Terror of Heinz Billig and the Desertion of Asangulow 99

Neu Turkestan and the Infamous Brigade "Dirlewanger" 101

Warsaw 105

Harun el-Raschid Bey and the Slovak Uprising . 115

Downfall in Lombardy 121

"Homeric Apologies". 129

History of the 13 Waffengebirgsdivision der SS
"Handschar" (Croat. No. 1) 131

"Skanderbeg" - the Albanian SS. 181

Resources 193

Internet/ Archives 199

Introduction

Anyone who thinks of the recruitment of Muslim volunteers for German military service in World War II will initially think of the mediagenic Bosnian volunteers in the "Handschar" division, with their famous "Fez" on their heads, or the units of the "Sonderverband Bergmann." The latter made history, especially due to their renowned commander, Theodor Oberländer. Under Adenauer, Oberländer even made it to a ministerial post. He was then harshly attacked by Moscow for his past as a foreman, in which he recruited Caucasian volunteers against communism.

But there was more going on than that, both within the regular German army and the SS. As the army focused on building legions and field battalions, it took the bulk of the volunteers under its wing. This made Heinrich Himmler, the Reichsführer-SS, realize there were unprecedented opportunities for his empire. Since the SS could not draw from Germany's youth limitlessly, enormous possibilities were to be found here. The German army entered the Caucasus in the summer of 1942. Thousands of Muslim Red Army soldiers could be recruited in the prisoner-of-war camps. The SS had already gained experience with volunteers who fought along in the "crusade against Bolshevism" through legions from Western countries. Himmler thought Islam would make for good soldiers who could fight against their common "Jewish enemy." In Himmler's eyes, the religion of Islam provided an excellent military posture since Islamists were willing to die for God and their homeland.

This view resulted in Himmler attempting to win Osttruppen for the Waffen-SS after the army had already tried to do the same. In doing so, he undermined the army shamelessly. The Third Reich was characterized by an entangled knot of often antagonistic agencies, and in this case, the SS and the army were also in each other's way. When success did not come, some specialists were even exchanged and dealt with harshly. Himmler was impatient, but this issue proved more challenging than he expected. The differences between the Germans and the Caucasus volunteers proved greater than he thought they would be. The same was true for the Bosnian Waffen-SS soldiers of the "Handschar" division. They had to be moved to France to rebuild in peace, which still did not prevent an uprising.

Despite all the studies, reports, and wise counsel, the construction of the Islamic Caucasus units,

Introduction

mostly Turkmen and Azerbaijanis, was quite difficult. Names were shuffled endlessly, and the "unit under construction" was moved from training camp to training camp. There was still no internal structure, despite all the goodwill from inspired officers such as Mayer-Mader, Hermann, and Hintersatz. This resulted in rebellion and desertions. Full deployment of the unit hardly came about. As punishment, draconian measures were taken. For a while, the "Ostmuselmanische" unit operated under the wings of the notorious brigade "Dirlewanger," which had a terrible reputation in operations against partisans behind the front lines. The Caucasian units thus found themselves caught up in the notorious "Kleinkrieg" behind the front lines, in the so-called Korpsrückwärts and occupied territories, where they fell under the command of the Höhere SS und Polizeiführer, men who had often washed their hands in the blood of the Holocaust.

The first part of this book follows the largest unit of Muslim Waffen-SS volunteers formed within the Waffen-SS. This unit was constantly given new names, but its nickname was the addition "Neu Turkestan." This sounds ambitious, which was also what men like Oberländer propagated. In addition to the military effort, the aim was to stimulate the aspirations of the "Ostvölker" to be autonomous. This would fuel the internal revolt against Moscow and communism. To this end, the support of the Grossmufti from Jerusalem was also employed. The SS found itself in a tricky position here. Indeed racial thinking compared awkwardly with the sovereignty wishes of Islam, although the SS certainly tried to compromise on religion. It is remarkable to see the bills for purchasing dozens of Korans, neatly paid for by the SS Hauptamt. But Himmler also had to reckon with Hitler, who was suspicious of practically all his allies and had a deep-seated contempt for Slavic men. Hitler did share the view that out of all the Soviet people, the Turkmen, who were not Slavic, were best suited as allies. The historically good relationship between Ankara and Berlin also played a role.

The history of "Neu Turkestan" is complicated for many reasons. The unit was too small to do proper monographic research. In addition, the source material is limited. We know very little about the final phase. The unit, and Himmler's plans with it, played no significant role within the mastodon of the Eastern Front. But the plans would have had potential had they been deployed earlier and executed with more tact and insight. There was a mutual interest alongside all the differences. It was the West that enslaved the Islamic people. Nazi Germany could have been the power that gave wind to the anti-co-

Introduction

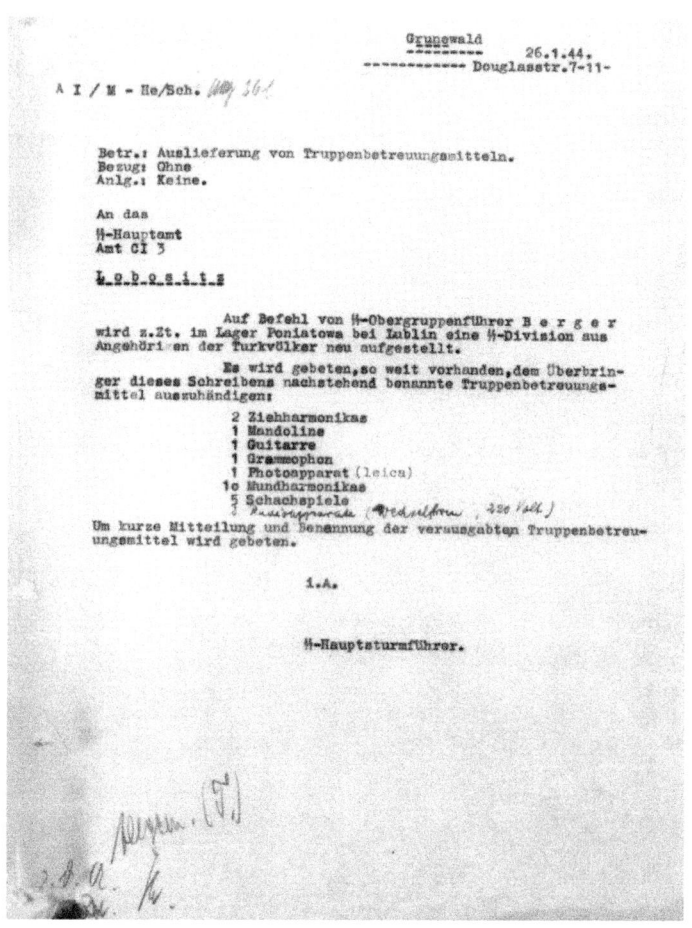

Alignment order from the SS-division by Gottlob Berger, head of the SS-Hauptamt

lonialist forces, just as the Soviet Union emerged after World War II as the advocate of liberation movements in Africa, Asia, and Central America. Stalin seized the opportunities which Hitler let slip. Muslims in the Balkans were also recruited. In the second part of this book, we will especially dwell on the "Handschar" division, which consisted of Bosnian Muslims. It was to be deployed against Tito and found its way to the Hungarian front lines at the end of the war. Here, too, the Nazis tried to build up reliable units with the help of the Grossmufti. But as with "Neu Turkestan," things were also unruly here. There were many misunderstandings, and Nazi ideology was difficult to reconcile with Islam. In relatively peaceful France, attempts were made to build "Handschar" into a reliable division. But there were also desertions in this case, and German officers were even murdered.

This history in this book can be read as the constantly abrasive development of an atypical product that nevertheless fought for its existence within Nazi Germany. In recent years, several studies have appeared that focus on the general relations between Islam and Nazism, and the Grossmufti and Nazi Germany. Also, the topic has value when looking at current affairs. The use of revolutionary movements and religion to change power relations is commonplace. A caliphate has recently emerged (and disappeared) in the Middle East, and Moscow struggles with the unruliness of Islam in old Soviet territories - think Crimean Tatars - and in Afghanistan. In the Cold War, the fueling of sovereignty thinking by the major powers played a prominent role on sever-

> **Merkblatt**
> **für das Verhalten gegenüber „Hilfswilligen"**
>
> 1. Die Bewährung landeseigener Einheiten im Partisanen- und Frontkampf rechtfertigt verstärkte Zulassung bzw. Anwerbung von Hilfswilligen aus den Kriegsgefangenen und den truppendiensttauglichen Männern vom Bolschewismus befreiten Zivilbevölkerung.
> 2. Die Heranziehung weiter Teile der Bevölkerung zum aktiven Kampf in den landeseigenen Einheiten und zur Mitarbeit hat neben dem militärischen den weiteren Vorteil, daß die beteiligten Hilfswilligen und ihre Angehörigen in eine Gegensatzstellung zum Bolschewismus kommen. Antibolschewistisch aufgeklärten Menschen werden den Juden niemals mehr trauen; sie sind endgültig kompromittiert.
> 3. Den deutschen Führern und vorgesetzten Dienststellen fällt die Aufgabe zu, aus den Freiwilligen zuverlässige Bundesgenossen Deutschlands zu machen, die am Ausgang des Kampfes entscheidend interessiert und gegenüber der bolschewistischen Propaganda gewappnet sind. Nur der zum Antibolschewismus erzogene Hilfswillige kann mit der Zeit ein vollwertiger Kamerad des nationalsozialistischen deutschen Soldaten werden im gemeinsamen Kampf gegen Judentum und Kapitalismus. Bei falscher Behandlung der Hilfswilligen selbst oder ihrer Angehörigen und Landsleute können sie jedoch zu einer Gefahr werden.
> 4. Die Verschiedenheit der Beweggründe zur freiwilligen Meldung, die zwischen materieller Grundlage (Söldnertyp) und ideeller Einstellung (antibolschewistischer Patriot) schwanken, macht die Lenkung und Betreuung der Hilfswilligen besonders schwierig und bedarf sorgfältiger Einfühlung in die Mentalität der Hilfswilligen. Persönlicher Haß und Rachsucht gegen die NKWD sind ebenfalls häufig; sie führen bei mangelnder Beaufsichtigung zu Grausamkeiten, die der Feind propagandistisch ausnützt und die auf die deutsche Wehrmacht zurückfallen.
> 5. Bei der Bewertung der Beweggründe zur freiwilligen Meldung ist allein die Frage des größten Nutzens für den Kampf gegen den Bolschewismus maßgebend. Zu- oder Abneigung gegenüber einzelnen Typen der Hilfswilligen ist falsche Sentimentalität. Bei nüchterner Wertung erweist es sich, daß sowohl Söldner als auch Idealisten Stärken und Schwächen haben.
> 6. Der Hilfswillige fordert von der Führung Gerechtigkeit, Organisationskraft, Verständnis und Fürsorge. Genügt seine Führung diesen Forderungen, so billigt er ihr Strenge zu, unterwirft sich Entbehrungen und erfüllt willig und ausdauernd hohe Leistungen.
> 7. Die deutschen Führer und Ausbilder der Hilfswilligen müssen bemüht sein, das Vertrauen der Hilfswilligen zu gewinnen. Niemals überheblich oder schroff auftreten. Fehler durch vorgesetzte Hilfswillige beseitigen und rügen lassen. Gegen Disziplinlosigkeit streng vorgehen, die verfügten Maßnahmen jedoch dem Betroffenen verständlich machen. Es empfiehlt sich, den Hilfswilligen die für bestimmte Vergehen vorgesehenen Strafen im voraus zu erklären. Sich überzeugen, daß die gegebenen Befehle sachlich und sprachlich verstanden werden. Überlautes Sprechen und Anschreien ist wirkungslos und verprellt den Russen.
> 8. Das Eingehen auf die Mentalität der Hilfswilligen und die Fürsorge für sie darf nicht zu übertriebener Vertrauensseligkeit und argloser Gutgläubigkeit führen. Einzelne Enttäuschungen sind mit Sicherheit zu erwarten (Agenten!); sie dürfen nicht entmutigen.
> 9. Schimpfworte und Fluchen sind zu vermeiden; sie gelten beim Russen als kulturlos und mindern seine Achtung vor dem Vorgesetzten. Körperliche Züchtigungen sind verboten. Auch vorgesetzten Hilfswilligen sind körperliche Züchtigungen gegen ihre Untergebenen zu untersagen.
> 10. Kriegsgefangene, die zu Hilfswilligen-Einheiten kommen, empfinden zuerst die Befreiung vom Druck des Gefangenenlagers am stärksten. Die Gefahr des Verbummelns in der freieren Atmosphäre ist gegeben. Für Beschäftigung auch außerhalb des Dienstes sorgen, Lässigkeiten ahnden, auf stramme Haltung und strenge Grußpflicht achten.

German protocol on how to deal with 'Hilfswilligen'

al continents, thinking that came forth out of their own ideological and geopolitical interests. With a bit of imagination, the Arab Spring could also be included in this category. In addition, the role of Islamic soldiers within the allied military has been in the spotlight in recent years. Their part in this has been pointed out with some force for the purpose

The SS got its recruts from the milions of Soviet war prisoners, among others. Here, the surrender of Soviet troops at the Krim

of connecting. This text may make clear that reality is more multiform.

Also, the plan of revolutionizing countries and regions was a proven German means of improving one's own strategic position and weakening the opponent. We can think of the Irish issue, the Zimmermann telegram, the Mexico-U.S. relationship, and, above all, the Russian Revolution. Financing and steering the train of revolutionaries toward St. Petersburg, the German interference was so great Lenin feared being called a German mercenary. The Communists used an intricate system of stooges to reduce any appearance of being precisely that. As we will see in the plans of Mayer-Mader and Oberländer, revolutionary plans in Central Asia played a significant role. There, they also wanted to mobilize expelled Soviet Muslims in Iraq and Iran for a holy war against Moscow. Islam as a weapon in a *proxy war*. Plans to revolutionize the Caucasus had already emerged in World War I, and these plans were revived in World War II.

This book focuses on the units "Neu Turkestan" and "Handschar" and all the perils that come with them. They are placed within the general development of the Osttruppen and - in a fleeting sense - its relationship to Islam as a whole. This makes it a small monograph on a small subject that could have become very large. The history library is filled with such poignant chapters full of human suffering. The unit members would live out their final days in the gulags of Stalinist Russia.

Dr. Perry Pierik

Neu Turkestan Division

The history of Muslim soldiers serving in the Waffen-SS took serious shape when it became the Ostmuselmanischen SS-Division. This unit, which started out as a regiment (and in practice hardly grew beyond it), constantly changed names in the German records: Ostmuselmanischen SS-Division, 1.regiment, 1.Ostmuselmansichen SS regiment, Neu Turkestan Division, 1.Muselmanischen SS Division Neu Turkestan, Ost-Mohammedanischen-SS-und-Polizei-Division and Osttürkischer Waffenverband der SS.[1] What the names had in

---

[1] The original documents surrounding this unit are mostly found on the microfilm roll T354 roll 161 in the National Archives in Washington, but also in the Bundesarchiv. The names mentioned occur in the approximately 700 pages of documentation. The variety came from a certain carelessness but also from the fact that the SS-Hauptamt and the Reichsführer-SS Heinrich Himmler were constantly changing plans. One moment they talked about a regiment, for example; in another, they expressed ambitions about it becoming a division, and even later, they spoke of a corps. There was also internal debate as to what the correct designation should be. It was SS-Sturmbannführer Brandenburg who came to the proposal Ost-Mohamedanische SS-und-Polizei-Division. The addition "Polizei" was not mentioned again in any other document.

common was that they were all designations for an initiative of the SS that began with a memo from Walter Schellenberg dated October 14th, 1943. In this memo, Schellenberg pointed out the possibilities for a Muslim legion for the Waffen-SS to the head of the SS, Hauptamt Gottlob Berger. Creating volunteer legions had already been done before, for example, for the Dutch, Flemish, Norwegians, Spaniards, and Baltic countries. Thus the advice joined an existing "tradition." In addition, the recruitment of Muslim soldiers, as well as Soviet residents in general, had been left to the army until then, which had employed large numbers of men using Hiwis, Bau, and Guard Battalions (Hiwa). Gottlob Berger brought this plan to the attention of the Reichsführer-SS. Heinrich Himmler, forever in competition with the army, suddenly saw growth opportunities for his Waffen-SS, the military branch of the SS empire.

Osttruppen

The history of the Ostmuselmanischen-SS unit is largely shrouded in mist. Even in George Tessin's great survey work, little or nothing was written about it. Little is also known about the much larger-scale deployment of "Ostvölker" in the army. The creation of the legions with "Ostvölker" for the army went back as far as late 1941, relatively soon after the Soviet invasion in June of that year. On their way there, they approached the Caucasus, although there were military setbacks near the city of Rostov. Among the millions of prisoners of war were many Muslim soldiers coming from the Caucasus region. As Muslims, they had a problematic relationship with the atheist Soviet regime. This led to the creation of units that would fight on the German side. All in all, about one million Soviet men conspired with the Germans. These included "Hiwis" (Hilfswilliger), local militias, "Volkswehren," "Sicherungsformationen," and combat units. Over time, the status of these men grew as they were increasingly seen as full-fledged German soldiers.

They were given full rights as well, especially where combat units were concerned. In addition, the Osttruppen were also increasingly able to lay claim to their national character, which gave them the position of "allies" rather than soldiers in German service. This also translated back into the organization of the Osttruppen, among the Cossacks, for example, who were given a "Chef der Hauptverwaltung der Kosakenheere." He, in turn, had his "Lord" under him: the Don Kosaken, Kuban Kosaken, Terek Kosaken, and the Sibert Kosaken, as well as under Generalleutnant Von Pannwitz the 1.Kosakendivision and later the XV.Kosaken Kavalleriekorps. The Armenians, Azerbaijanis, North Caucasians, Turkestan, and Volga-Tatar units had their own legions. Separate Crimean-Tatar formations were added to these as well as the so-called Kalmückenverband Dr. Doll, from which the Kalmükisches Cavalerie Korps would grow. Ukrainian volunteers were given their own "liberation units" and Waffen-SS division. Russians and Belarusians served in the Russian Liberation Army of General Andrei Andreyevich Vlassov. Vlassov became a German prisoner of war after the battle in the Wolchov Kessel and defected to the Germans. This Russian Liberation Army, ROA, was supported by a political body - the Committee to Liberate the People of Russia (KONR) - and consisted of several divisions. The XV.Kosaken Kavallerie Corps and the Kalmuckian "Verband" also merged into the ROA, which went down in Prague and the Czech Republic in 1945.

Kleinkrieg and Kosakentum

Initially, the units were planned for guard duties and deployment behind the front lines. One of the earliest mentions of Osttruppen deployment must be on September 4th, 1941, of a battalion of Estonians. On November 25th of that year, we encounter the "Schutzmannschafts-Abteilungen" in the documents, in the area of Heeresgruppe Nord. The situation along the front lines of the enclosed city of Leningrad continued to play out, and the Soviets launched heavy offensives time and again to break through the ring of encirclement that was starving the city. The Germans were forced to deploy the "Osttruppen" directly in the front line also. They generally did well, but the German press initially gave them little credit for this. When the commander of the German 18th Army on the northern part of the Eastern Front, General Lindemann, wanted to compliment the "Osttruppen," he was reprimanded by Heeresgruppe commander Von Küchler.

The setbacks that kept coming for the German army and the demanding occupation "Alltag" made

Kozakken officer

the urgency of the Osttruppen increasingly more evident. In the hinterland, the Germans were particularly troubled by the partisans becoming more active. This had begun in the fall of 1941 and would burden the German troops more and more. The "Kleinkrieg" this entailed was bloody and caused much unrest, even among the civilian population. They were often caught between German occupiers and partisans living off the land. It was a logical step for the Germans to fall back on the "Kosakentum," which had experience with the "Kleinkrieg" and had traditionally stayed far away from communism. The Cossacks had long resisted and were therefore recruited as a priority by the Germans. Lieutenant Von Kleist was employed to search the various POW camps for Cossacks in order to recruit them

Kozakken in German service

for the German army. These activities started around October 6th, 1941. Not much later, Cossacks were deployed in "Hundertschaften" in the German "Sicherungsdivisionen." These were divisions that were deployed behind the front lines in the areas that fell under the command of the army (Korück= Korpsrückwärts) and with the regular troops.

Hitler: "We Will Never Create a 'Russian Army'"

Hitler's attitude toward these initiatives was duplicitous. He remarked that Germany would "never create a 'Russian army'" on June 8th, 1943, to his confidant in the OKW (Oberkommando der Wehrmacht), General Wilhelm Keitel. However, developments to that end were already underway. Hitler was reluctant to openly recognize their deployment, possibly because he feared the political consequences. After all, historically, territorial claims were often paid for in blood. For this reason, Hitler himself initially hesitated to deploy Romanians and Hungarians. These were allies and not "Osttruppen." It was interesting, however, that Hitler, like Himmler with his Ostmuselmanischen troops, considered the Turkish people the most suitable. According to Hitler, they were the furthest away from Bolshevism and Moscow, citing their actions in the 19th century against the Russians under Imam Samil. The relationship between Germany and Turkey also played a role. They had been allies in World War I, and in this sense, they had a moral and emotional alliance. The historian Joachim

Hoffmann argues that this went so far that the Germans were hesitant to deploy Georgian and Armenian units, not wanting to antagonize the Turkish people and Ankara. The German ambassador in Turkey, the cunning political fox Franz von Papen, constantly pointed this out. He referred to Turkey's centuries-long pioneering role in the Arab world by stating that in any solution to the Arab question, "Turkey must not be forgotten."

The Turkmen were known as warlike people. In World War I, they served the Czar in cavalry units. In World War II, in addition to the Osttruppen in German service, about 300,000 Turkmen served in the Soviet Army, of whom about 100,000 died. One of the Soviet Union's first heroes in 1941 was a Turkmen, Kurban Durdy. The Turkmen served in specific Red Army units, such as the 33rd Independent Mortar Brigade, the 98th and 188th Infantry Brigades, the 63rd and 81st Cavalry Divisions, and the 18th and 21st Mountain Cavalry Divisions. Many units were deployed at Stalingrad.

The relationship chilled when the odds of war turned in the summer of 1943. Turkey distanced itself by taking down an Arab pro-German spy network, among other things. Attempts were made to form a new network through contacts of Jerusalem's Grossmufti, El-Hoesseini.

Hitler: "We Will Never Create a 'Russian Army'"

The "Hundertschaften" of the Cossacks was soon copied to other groups, including groups from the Caucasus. These were mostly deployed for training within the framework of the 444th Sicherungsdivision (8th Army) and later with the 454th Sicherungsdivision. Both operated on the southern part of the Eastern Front and were used in anti-Partisan activities in General Karl von Roques' Korück area.

Mayer-Mader and the Turkmen Troops

The first serious encounter with Turkmen forces occurred under the auspices of Major Andreas Mayer-Mader. He was working for the Abwehr, the intelligence service commanded by Admiral Wilhelm Canaris. Mayer-Mader was deeply involved in the fate of the Turkmen, and he spoke several of their dialects. He had been a military adviser to Chiang Kai-shek in China and was now pushing for an independent Turkmen state in Central Asia, separate from the Soviet Union. He advocated his idea to the Amt Ausland/Abwehr II because he considered this endeavor important in light of the German plans to dismantle the Soviet Union. In doing so, Mayer-Mader cooperated with the migrant Uzbek politician Veli Kajum-chan, who would later become president of the "Nationalturkestanischen Einheitskomitee." This "committee" was, in effect, an exile government of the yet-to-be-established Turkmen state. In preparation, under the wings of the Abwehr, units had already been set up. Their main focus was not so much military but rather sabotage and intelligence. These units were trained at the Truppenübungsplatz Rembertow in occupied Poland (General Gouvernement), a former Russian artillery training ground. All this was hidden behind the name "Abwehrunternehmen Tiger B."

The creation of the Turkestan infantry battalion 450 also led to the deployment of Turkmen combat troops. Mayer-Mader had assigned officer positions to Turkish soldiers. This provided a reliable combat unit that held its own against stronger partisan divisions in the Gluchov and Jampol areas. However, the Germans who held leadership positions felt disadvantaged, and tensions arose. Eventually, Mayer-Mader, who was seen as a "father," left his post and was replaced by Major Bergen, who had to end the "Asian relationships" within the battalion. His position after this was difficult. His fellow officers referred to him as "the Chinese major," preferring to deal with Kazakhs and Kyrgyz instead of with German officers. This was one of the reasons Mayer-Mader would later try his luck again in the SS.

Professor Oberländer and the "Sonderverband Bergmann"

The influence of Professor Oberländer was also of importance. This professor of economics and agriculture, attached to the universities of Königsberg, Greifswald, and Prague, was also a reserve officer in the OKW Ausland/Abwehr II and a Caucasus specialist. As Abwehrman, he maintained good connections with the staff of Heeresgruppe Süd (Oberst Winter). In October 1941, they agreed that it would be useful, in view of an upcoming summer field trip in 1942, to have their own native units at their disposal. Here, Oberländer could draw on previous experience he had gained with Ukrainian volunteers in the unit "Nachtigall." This unit, "Bataillon Ukrainische Gruppe Nachtigall," had already been established in February 1941, before the invasion in cooperation with Ukrainian nationalists hostile to Moscow. Together with the unit "Roland," they were under the control of the Lehrregiment "Brandenburg z.b.V. 800", which was under the Abwehr (Canaris). Together, the units formed the Ukrainian Legion. They would later form the nucleus of the 14th Ukrainian Waffen-SS Division "Galizien."

Oberländer's efforts led to the creation of a collection unit where the nationalities were organized based on their company, the so-called Sonderverband Bergmann. This 2,300-man unit was transferred to Mittenwald for mountain training and did good service with Heeresgruppe A (which had invaded the Caucasus). Meanwhile, Oberländer had become increasingly at odds with the SS, particularly over the brutal German occupation policy. After spending some time assembling Turk battalions, he was pushed aside. The army had also tried to incorporate the Abwehreen unit through the 162nd I.D., commanded by Colonel Oskar Ritter von Niedermayer. Intervention by Abwehrchef Wilhelm Canaris prevented this at the last moment. Via Mayer-Mader, it now came to training the "Ostvölker" in the Generalgouvernement. With this, the leading body, "Kommando der Ostlegionen" (initially called "Aufstellungsstab den Ostlegionen"), was established on January 23rd, 1943. The training center Rembertów (later Radom) was its central point, which in turn, starting January 1st, 1944, fell under the "General der Freiwilligen Verbände im OKH (Oberkommando des Heeres)," General Ernst-August Köstring. The military diplomat, who spoke Russian, was a Caucasus expert. He had put himself in the spotlight by winning over the Karatschaiern to the German cause. His speech at an

Islamic folk festival was appreciated so much that he was taken on the shoulders and thrown in the air three times, as was customary. Starting in June 1943, he was an inspector with the Turkmen until his new appointment in January 1944.

The Turkestan Legion was the first to be assembled, followed by the Caucasian Legion in January 1942. The basis for the first unit was the Turk Battalion 450, which Mayer-Mader spearheaded. This unit was transferred to the Waffen-SS when Mayer-Mader was later appointed to the SS. Kyrgyz, Uzbeks, Khazars, Tajiks, and Turkmen served in this unit. New legions rapidly emerged: the "Caucasian-Mohammedanian" legion under Major Riedel, the "Georgian" legion under Hauptmann Houselle, later Oberleutnant Breitner, and the "Armenian" legion under Hauptmann Kucera. A Volga-Tatar legion was added on August 15th, 1942. During August 1942, the formation of legions looked as follows:

1) Turkestanischen Legion in Legionowo
2) Kaukasisches Mohammedanische Legion in Jedlnia
3) Nordkaukasisches Legion in Wesola
4) Georgisches Legion in Kruszyna
5) Armenische Legion in Pulawy
6) Wolgatatarische Legion in Jedlnia

General Olbricht characterized the units as "Verbände freiwilliger Kämpfer für die Befreiung ihrer Heimat vom Bolschewismus und für die Freiheit ihres Glaubens." The bulk of the volunteers were used in the Generalgouvernement as field battalions. A total of 53 battalions were formed, with a total strength of about 53,000 men.

The Collaboration with the Crimean Tatars

In addition, there were Crimean Tatar units in the 11th Army, commanded by the Einsatzgruppe D of ss-Oberfüher Ohlendorf. This means the Islamic volunteers collaborated directly with a vital division of the "Holocaust by bullets." The Crimean Tatars were brutally persecuted and oppressed by Stalin, and thousands fled to Turkey during Soviet times. For many Crimean Tatars, the German occupation came as a liberation. A liberation committee was formed in Simferopol, Crimea's capital. Photos show a swastika flag flying on the minaret of the mosque. On January 18th, 1942, the OKH gave way to cooperating with the Crimean Tatars, who were very sensitive to this idea. In 1941, between 179,000 and 225,000 Crimean Tatars were in "German hands," and they reported en masse for German service. In total, some 200,000 young men would enlist, which constituted a considerable percentage of collaboration.

The Tatars were so reliable that they were not first sent to the Generalgouvernement for training and drill but deployed right away. The Crimean Tatars guarded their own villages and towns and helped fight the partisans very effectively. For the Einsatzgruppe, they were an important ally when Ohlendorf destroyed the 45,000- to 65,000-strong Jewish community in Crimea. Von Manstein's 11th Army had insisted on urgency because of the food shortage. During this research, direct involvement in the Jewish execution was not found, but like the 11th Army, the Crimean Tatars helped facilitate it. Anti-Partisan actions also caused large-scale fighting. More than 400 Crimean Tatars were wounded in these battles.

The number of 53 battalions would continue to grow. The total number remains vague. In the annotation to the Lagebesprechungen in Führerhauptquartier, American sources were cited. These sources name 184 battalions (including many non-Islamic). According to a survey by the Ostministerium on January 24th, 1945, the number of men from the "Ostvölker" serving in armed units amounted to nearly 600,000 men. This included everything: the army, Waffen-SS, police, border guards, ROA, and SS legions. This gave the following picture:

The Collaboration with the Crimean Tatars

Kalmück rider

- Lithuanians: 36,800
- Latvians   104,000
- Estonians   10,000
- Turk-Tatars   20,550
- Crimean Tatars   10,000
- Armenians   7,000
- Azerbaijanis   36,500
- Georgians   19,000
- Kalmücken   5,000
- North Caucasian legion 15,000
- Russians (ROA).   310,000

Total: 573,850 troops

Kalmücken in German military service

In addition, hundreds of thousands more Hiwis served. General Zeitzler reported to Hitler in the "Lagebesprechung" of June 8th, 1943, that on that date, about 220,000 Hiwis were serving in the German armed forces and occupation units.

Merkblatt für Tatarenschulung. Nr. 1.

Weshalb müssen die Tataren mit uns kämpfen?

I. Die Verbrechen des Bolschewismus am Tatarentum.

1) Durch den Bolschewismus ist die Krim und damit das Tatarentum in grösste Not versetzt worden. Bedenkenlos sind Vorräte in grössten Mengen vernichtet worden, Industrieanlagen gesprengt, ohne dass sich die sowjetischen Machthaber auch nur im geringsten um das Schicksal der Bevölkerung gekümmert hätten.

Ein Beweis dafür, dass am Bolschewismus nur seine Machthaber ein Interesse haben, niemals das Volk.

Infolge der bolschewistischen Zerstörungen ist in manchen Teilen der Krim Lebensmittelmangel eingetreten. Nach dem Völkerrecht ist ein Siegerstaat keineswegs verpflichtet, die Bevölkerung des eroberten Staates zu ernähren. Das deutsche Oberkommando in der Krim tut aber das möglichste, der Bevölkerung zu helfen. Es leistet überall in der Wirtschaft aufbauende Arbeit, nicht zerstörende.

2) Jede Rückkehr des Bolschewismus würde nur weitere Zerstörungen bedeuten. Das beweist die Tätigkeit der Partisanen, die immer wieder den Versuch machen—soweit sie noch die Möglichkeit haben—die Tatarendörfer in den Bergen zu überfallen und auszurauben, dabei aber grosse Worte von der Befreiung der Krim im Munde führen. Es kann gar kein Zweifel daran bestehen, das der Kommunismus das Tatarentum am liebsten ganz vernichten würde, falls er wieder zur Macht kommen würde.

3) Das Sowjetsystem hat während seines Bestehens dauernd das tatarische Volk seiner besten Kräfte beraubt. Zuletzt unter dem Schlagwort der Entkulakisierung. Angeblich sollten damit nur die reichen Leute mit unverdientem Wohlstande beseitigt werden. In Wahrheit wurde damit überall die örtliche Intelligenz ausgerottet. Die Moskauer Juden wollten keine unbequemen Leute im Wege haben, wenn sie daran gingen, Land und Volk auszubeuten. Mit einer führerlosen, ungebildeten Masse konnten sie natürlich leichter umgehen.

4) Aus demselben Grunde wurde die Religion beseitigt. Nicht deswegen allein, weil die Mollahs, die islamischen Geistlichen, materiell besser standen.

Die Religion war ein Bollwerk gegen den seelenlosen Materialismus Sie gab dem Volke inneren Halt. Die mohammedanischen Geistlichen konnten auch niemals den Juden als politischen oder wirtschaftlichen Führer anerkennen. Infolgedessen wurden die Geistlichen beseitigt oder verbannt.

5) Das Land wurde den Bauern weggenommen. Trotz des Widerstandes der Tataren wurden Zehntausende von Judenfamilien aus der Ukraine und Weissrussland auf tatarischem Lande angesiedelt.

II. Was gibt Deutschland dafür dem tatarischen Volk?

1) Der Nationalsozialismus sieht die Nationen als göttliche Einrichtung an, während der Bolschewismus nur einen Völkerbrei anstrebt.

2) Deutschland gewährleistet dem tatarischen Volk freie Entwicklung der arteigenen Kultur der Tataren, tastet die altüberkommenen Sitten und Gebräuche nicht an.

German view of the Tataars – German collaboration

National Identity, Liberation Armies, and the German Occupation Policy

The developments concerning the "Ostvölker" were followed with interest by the Führer's headquarters, but also with a certain distance. The various services were operating more or less on their own. For example, Keitel cited Rosenberg's Ostministerium several times when mentioning, "that's what they call so-and-so over there." As if they were completely new concepts; the national committees and liberation armies. Hitler, Zeitzler, and Keitel mainly debated the national character and to what extent political ambitions could arise from it. The latter, of course, was also dangerous for German purposes. They drew the line between the propagandistic value and reality.

The battalion structure, consisting of small units, was also retained for security reasons. "I believe a confederation to be completely incorrect," Zeitzler mused. "Battalions are still manageable; we can control them." He continued by saying, "An exception is the 'Kosakendivision,' which is very orderly." Hitler also made an exception for the Turkish people. "If we are successful in the Caucasus, we can obtain units not so much from the Georgians but from the Turkmen." According to Keitel: "They are an exception because they are the greatest enemies of Bolshevism." Nevertheless, the conversation on June 8th, 1943, closed with a warning. "Das Ausbauen ist schon gefährlich," Hitler stated, and so did Zeitzler: "It is becoming too much." Keitel warned of the "General der Osttruppen" favoring expansion. To this, Zeitzler reassured him: "No, I'll keep them in check. By no means. Battalions are the largest units."

But reality and wishful thinking began to be at odds. Even the future initiatives of Himmler, who wanted to build an entire SS corps (!) out of Turkmen, would push the wishes of the Nazi leadership. In many ways, the thousands of "Ostvölker" helping functioned as the lubricant of the "overstretched" German occupation. Any document from Heeresgruppe A clarifies to what extent the Army Group Süd (which had already split due to Stalingrad and the Caucasus operation) at least partly turned on the "Ostvölker." A document dated April 5th, 1943, gave the following picture:

17th Army Turkest.Feld Btl. 452 (250 men at 97th I.D.)
Aserb.Feld-Btl. I./73 (800 men near Taman)
Georg.Feld-Btl.I/9 (250 men at 9th I.D.)

Befehlshaber Strasse Kertsch: Aserb.Feld-Btl. 805 (300 men in Kolonka near Höhere Pi (pioneer) Führer, river transition Kertsch

Turkest.Feld-Btl. 811 (350 men, of which 150 Turkest, 130 Wolgatataren, 60 NordKaukasier, and 19 Georgians at the river crossing Kertsch)

Georg.Feld-Btl. II/4 (800 men river crossing Kertsch)

Georg.Feld-Btl. 796 (200 men water crossing Kertsch)

Befehlshaber der Krim, unit "Bergmann" (700 Georgians, 600 Azerbaijanis, 400 Nordcaucasians, 100 Armenians) at Kokkos, on the street to Simferopol-Yalta

Aserb.Feld-Btl.804 (800 men Zarigol near Feodosia)

Aserb.Feld-Btl.806 (600 men in Feodosia)

Stab Von Kleist: Turkes.Feld.Btl. 450 (700 men at Cherson)

Turkest.Btl. 370 (not legible) (300 Turkest. and 100 Wolgatatars)

Turkst.Feld-Btl. 781 (350 men at Cherson)

Turkst.Feld-Btl. 788 (250 men Cherson)

Nordkauk.Feld-Btl. 800 (300 men at Cherson)

Nordkauk.Feld.Btl. 801 (230 men Cherson)

Arm.Feld-Btl. 809 (400 men at Cherson unit later merged into "Bergmann")

Aserb.Feld-Btl.1/811 (580 men at Cherson)

Georg.Feld-Btl.795 (250 men at Cherson)

In addition to their own officers, there was German tribal personnel in the units, of course. To get an idea of the proportions, see the overview below of the formations of these units in the Generalgouvernement on April 14th, 1943:

Armen.Feld-Btl. 809: 34 Germans and 426 legionaries
Turkest.Feld-Btl. 781: 35 Germans and 319 legionaries
Turkest.Feld-Btl. 782: 18 Germans and 256 legionaries
Nordkauk.Feld-Btl. 800: 29 Germans and 357 legionaries
Georg. Feld-Btl. 795: 43 Germans and 253 legionaries
Aserb.Feld-Btl. 805: 29 Germans and 330 legionaries

According to the regulations, there were to be 52 German employees per battalion. In practice, this proved to be very minimal. In an internal memo dated May 1st, 1943, Generalleutnant Heinz Hellmich suggested to the General der Osttruppen to increase this to 95 men. Hellmich also noted that the Turkmen were eager to be equipped with German weapons because they had "no confidence in Russian weaponry." The Turkmen's distrust of the Bolsheviks ran deep. And they were not the only ones; non-Islamic units, such as the Kosaken Divison, also opted for German armament. As a result, the original Russian armament was used less and distributed among the other new units of Heeresgruppe A, which weren't always happy with it either.

Oberländer and the Conflict About the Murders in Taman

There were also major problems. Hellmich reported about evacuated relatives of "Ost-Freiwilligen" who were not doing well in Ukraine. They were treated miserably there. In messages to their fighting relatives, they wrote they were starving and were not allowed to grow food. As a response, soldiers insisted on leaving to help their families.

The harsh and racist German occupation policy did not help either. Oberländer, as commander of the "Bergmann" unit, reported on February 6th, 1943, that he was shocked at how Soviet prisoners of war were treated and how this was affecting the population and the "Osttruppen." Mass prisoners were forced to join in foot marches from Salawi-Janskaya to Temrjuk on the Taman Peninsula (east of the Kertsch Strait). Those who could not come along were simply shot. This was done brutally, according to Oberländer. Dozens at a time lay by the roadside while still alive. The locals gathered around them and were outraged by the treatment. Osttruppen in the region were also appalled. In ten

Theodor Oberländer

minutes time, Oberländer also saw at least three cases where the German guards looted the shot soldiers. They claimed they received orders to do so. Oberländer pointed out that "in any case, one has to execute the fallen out properly, so they are dead." He was also shocked that the executions took place in villages and towns where everyone could see it and where it "could be used for enemy propaganda." Oberländer concluded that the defection to and sympathy for the partisans would only grow this way.

Oberländer frustration about the situation was also evident in a second letter addressed to the "Kommandeur der Kriegsgefangenen im Operationsgebiet" dated March 30th, 1944. In it, he stated that he had seen at least "200 corpses" in the region in the days in question and that the guilty German guards were probably connected with DULAG 183 (Durchgangslager). Near Korschewski, another significant incident almost happened when 25 men could not continue, and German escorts threatened to shoot. Villagers and men from the 3rd Company "Bergmann" took care of the weakened soldiers. Six days later, they recuperated and were able to get to the DULAG on their own. "The damage caused by these incidents," Oberländer evaluated in his letter, "has not been repaired to this day."

But the unit also had a blind spot when it came to damaging morale. In a letter written by Major Bake on December 13th, 1942, who had to set up the "Ost-Ersatz-Truppenteil" at Baksan and Naltschik, this officer reported to Heeresgruppe A about his visit to the Georgian (Rest) Btl. 795 at Nowo Uruch. The unit had been in combat with three Soviet battalions and was struggling. The soldiers only had 18 rounds of ammunition per rifle, which was insufficient to engage in real combat. According to Bake, the Georgians had been plundered by the "Bergmann" unit, which had visited the battalion for inspection. They had taken the best men, horses, and equipment. Battalion 805 encountered Bake between Shemgala and Noshniy-Shemgale in a former Soviet penal camp, which did not look great either. On the way, Bake's car got stuck in the swampy ground. Still, Major Rank ("Gruppe Rank") tried to keep up the spirit. Rank asked for reinforcements to deal with the partisans in his area. He was also under a lot of work pressure because he was also temporarily serving in Battalion 809 (commanded by Officer Chalfaev).

Robbery of units took place elsewhere too. On January 23rd, seven Cossacks in Kirpilskaya were reported to have been raided by the 85th Azerbaijani Battalion. Uniform items, horses, food, and cutlery were stolen.

The documents contain numerous examples of the problems the Germans had with their new allies. Sometimes the cases were serious. In a field court at Feldausbildungsregiment 23, nine Azerbaijani volunteers were tried, for example, including deputy company commander Hassan Abdulasimow and Mohamed Mamedow of Azerbaijani battalion 804. They were sentenced to death for building a communist cell. Upon the Soviet landing at Fedosia, this cell would defect to the Red Army. They were also alleged to have contacted Commissioner Kusniczow's partisan group operating in the area. The consequences were severe once the Germans discovered this. The entire battalion was taken out of service and disarmed. They obviously weren't feeling secure anymore.

Theodor Oberländer in uniform

Islamic soldiers serving in the Waffen-SS

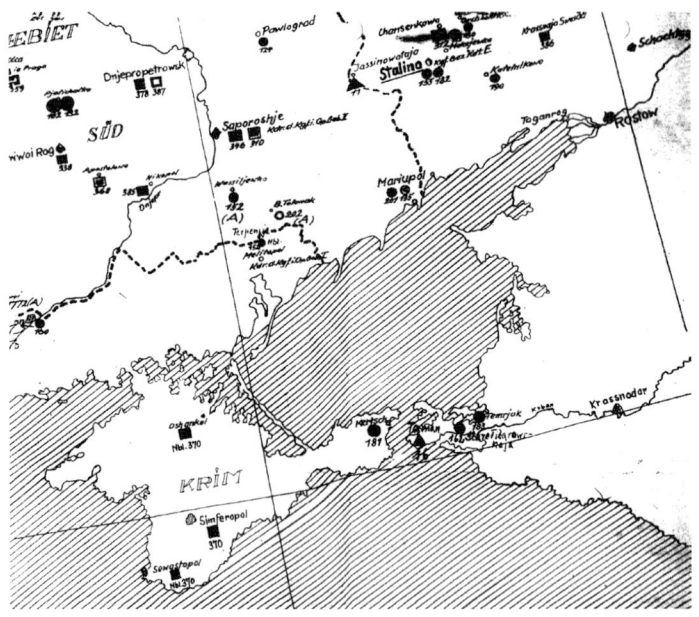

Area where the abuse of the Soviet war prisoners took place, which Oberländer reported

The battle itself was also taking its toll. A March 20th, 1943 report spoke of 10 to 25% "blutige Verluste" when it came to deploying the Turkmen battalions. Another 10 to 30% lost their units and were sometimes temporarily absorbed into German units. Five to 10% of them suddenly joined Baubataljons. Some even disappeared behind barbed wire again. The materials weren't up to standing either. Especially boots and pants were worn out, according to the "General der Osttruppen" on February 27th. Ninety to 100 percent of the heavy equipment was wasted either way. However, there wasn't much to begin with.

```
Sonderverband " Bergmann "          O.U., den 17. 4. 1943
Feldpost - No. 39 180

An
153. Feldausbildungsdivision

nachrichtlich: an Heeresgruppe A /IaF .

Mitte Dezember 1942 wurden vom Sonderverband " Bergmann "
folgende Offiziersanwärter zum 12. O.A.-Lehrgang gesandt:

    Feldw. Möllhoff
    Uffz.  Dr. Richter
    Uffz.  Gregersen
    Uffz.  v. Kruska
    Uffz.  Semmler
    Uffz.  Hackl .

Die Offiziersanwärter wurden zum Lehr-Rgt. "Brandenburg"
z.b.V. 800, Brandenburg/Havel als dem damaligen Heimat-
truppenteil in Marsch gesetzt. Von dort aus kamen sie zur
14.Erg. Kompanie nach Baden bei Wien zu einer kurzen Vor-
bereitung, um dann nach Ohrdruf zum 12. Waffenlehrgang
für Offiziersanwärter kommandiert zu werden. Da in der
Zwischenzeit der Sonderverband " Bergmann" aus der Unter-
stellung O.K.W./Abw.II ausschied und O.K.H. unterstellt
wurde, schied der Sonderverband "Bergmann" auch aus dem
Sonderverband "Brandenburg" aus. Eine Rückfrage bei Schule
4 für O.A. der Infanterie Thörn Süd 6 ergab, daß die vor-
stehend angeführten O.A. am 1.3.43 an Erg.Abt. Verband 805
des Sonderverbandes "Brandenburg" Havel in Marsch gesetzt
wurden. Obgleich der jetzige zustehende Ersatztruppenteil
Geb.Jäg.Ers.Rgt. 136, Innsbruck ist. Es besteht von hier
aus die Befürchtung, daß die Offiziersanwärter von Sonder-
verband "Brandenburg" festgehalten und für eigene Zwecke
verwendet werden. Da der Sonderverband "Bergmann" die
Offiziersanwärter, die voraussichtlich in Kürze Offiziere
werden, dringend für die Ausbildung und Führung des eigenen
Verbandes benötigt und die Offiziersanwärter außerdem aus
den Reihen der Unteroffiziere des Sonderverbandes "Bergmann""
hervorgegangen sind, bitten wir den Sonderverband "Branden-
burg" aufzufordern, die Offiziersanwärter sofort nach hier
in Marsch zu setzen.

                                    Oberländer
                        Hauptmann u. Führer des Sonderverbandes

Wegen Dringlichkeit der Angelegenheit sofort an
Heeresgruppe A /IaF. Zweiter Durchschlag über
153. Feldausbildungsdivision folgt.
```

Cooperation of 'Brandenburg' and 'Bergmann' 17 april 1943

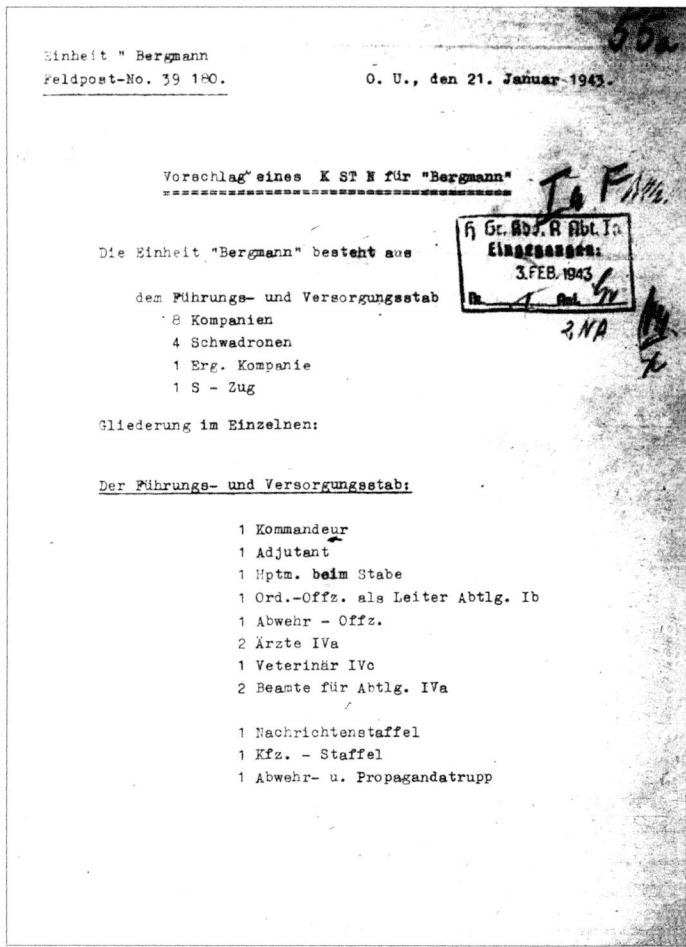

Unit 'Bergmann' 21 january 1943

```
Oberkommando der Heeresgruppe A					H.Qu., 17.4.1943
	Ia Nr. ___ /43 geh.
```

Betr.: Landsmannschaftliche Ärmelabzeichen für **turkestanische**
und **kaukasische Einheiten**

		An den
			Befehlshaber der Krim

Die für turkestanische und kaukasische Bataillone bezw. Kompanien gemäss Verfügung OKH/GenStdH/O.Qu.4/Ausb.Abt./Org.Abt. (II) Nr.2380/42 g.Kdos vom 2.6.1942 eingeführten landsmannschaftlichen Ärmelabzeichen sind von den Angehörigen des Sonderverbandes "Bergmann" (deutsches Rahmenpersonal und Legionäre) gemäss der landsmannschaftlichen Gliederung in Bataillone und Kompanien (Armenier, Aserbeidschaner, Georgier, Nordkaukasier) anzulegen. Die Abzeichen sind auf dem rechten Ärmel zu tragen.

Anforderungen auf Lieferung der Ärmelabzeichen sind durch Sonderverband "Bergmann" und bei vorliegendem Bedarf durch sämtliche turkestanischen und kaukasischen Einheiten an OKH/Chef H Rüst und BdE/AHA Ia (VI) zu richten.

				Für das Oberkommando der Heeresgruppe
					Der Chef des Generalstabes

Braclets for the voluntary units

Oberländer and the Conflict About the Murders in Taman

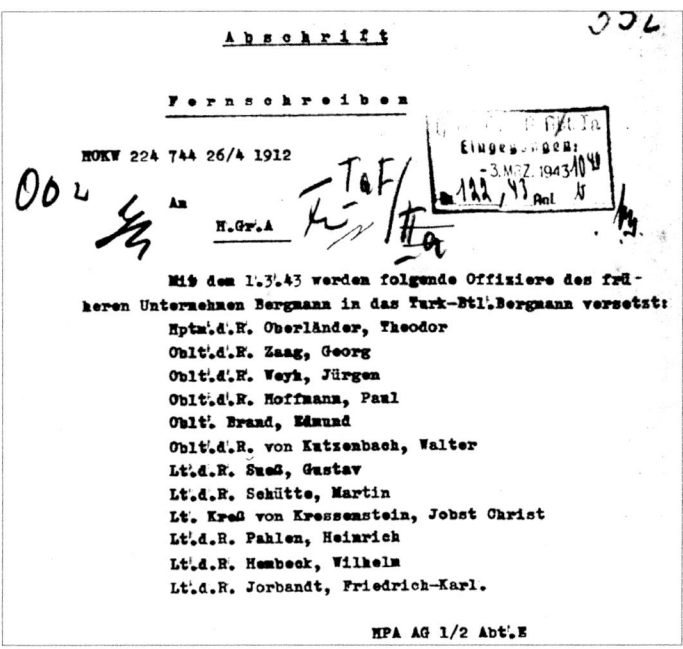

Officers for unit 'Bergmann'

Construction of unit 'Bergmann'

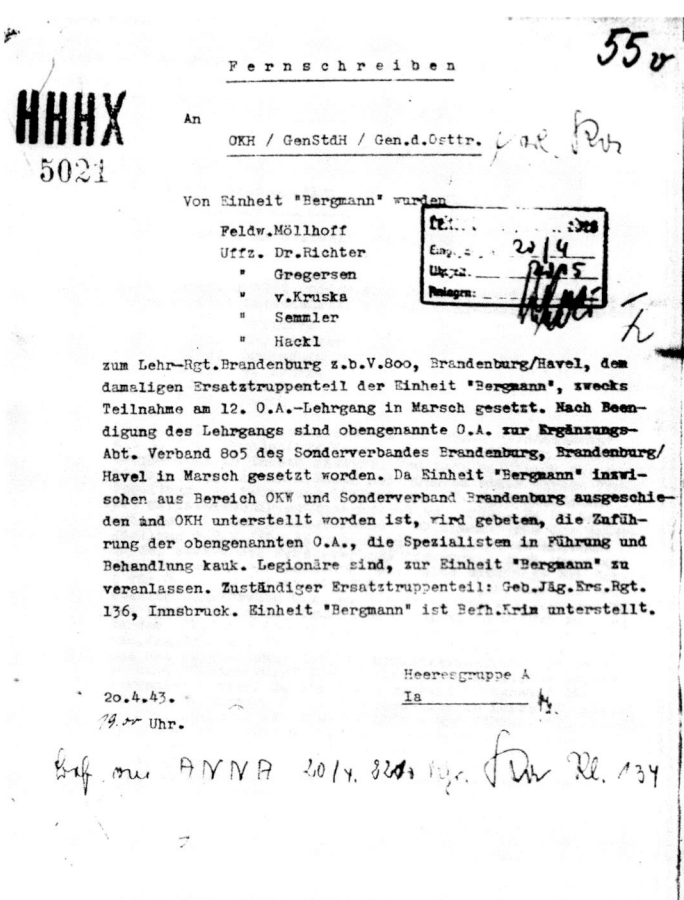

The Germans invested in the education of their volunteers

Propaganda - Caucasian Journalists in Dabendorf

Another growing concern for the Germans was the Soviets also recruiting their own "Osttruppen." A report by the intelligence service Fremde Heere Ost dated April 7th, 1943, made an initial inventory of these new troops. There were rumors about drafting a Polish army which seemed rather unlikely to the intelligence service because the exiled government in England would be against it. The Fremde Heere Ost was wrong in this case, for these units would be there. So would Czech units, Estonian, Latvian, and Lithuanian, ranging from division to corps to even army level.

To mobilize one's own "Osttruppen," propaganda was important. A journalism course was held in Dabendorf, Berlin, to which Eastern European journalists were invited. Thus, on March 30th, a list of 16 eligible candidates was drawn up. These were mostly people from Crimea and its surroundings. Some were already journalists in Simferopol and Melitopol, like Leonid Polski, Andrej Beskrowny and Boris Schirjajew, Nikolaj Derbuschew, Wjatscheslaw Radin, Jerim Piskunow, Boris Dsugajhew,

Viktor Surmenidi, and Valentin Nikitin. Two others, Nikolay Schubin and the already mentioned Beskrowny, also had "Cossack" indicated as their occupation. Their ages ranged from 18 (Vlanetin Nikitin) to 45 (Alexander Michailow). Their own newspapers, such as Dobrowolez (the Volunteer), reported on the Osttruppen's actions. Initially, they would print 3,600 copies per week.

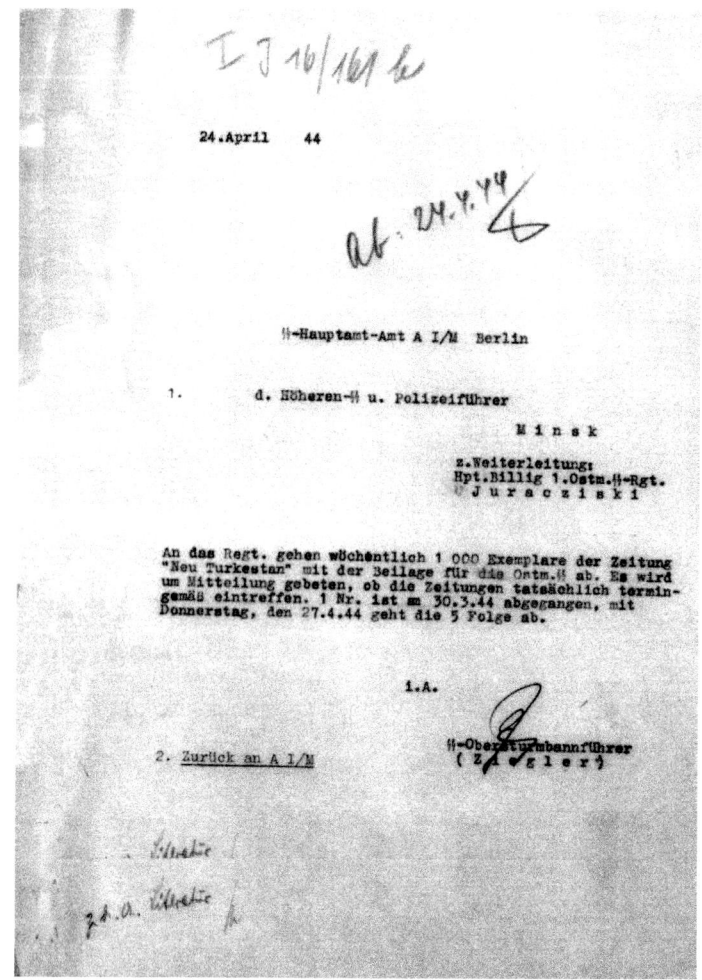

Correspondence around the periodic 'Neu Turkestan', april 1944

Islamic soldiers serving in the Waffen-SS

Azerbaijani periodic

Writings, Memos, and the 24 Theses of Oberländer

Many agencies and individuals wrote "Denkschriften" and internal memos about the new allies and how to deal with them. The offices of the Waffen-SS partly initiated this. Still, there were also conflicting opinions, such as that of Oberländer, who was considered too lenient by the Nazi leadership regarding the nationality issues of the Osttruppen. Oberländer thought along the same lines as Canaris (Abwehr) and the former ambassador Graf Schulenburg, who tried to correct the catastrophic German "Ostpolitik." This was no easy task. The various reports Oberländer wrote on this subject show he had a vision and a deep understanding of the region, but they were difficult to sell. We know from a close associate of Canaris that Hitler only got his hands on the report "24 Thesen zur Lage" (March 15th, 1943) "after much difficulty."

To gain insight into the lingering problems concerning the Osttruppen and later the Waffen-SS, it is good to name the "Thesen," or "theories," briefly. Freely translated:

1) People "called" to rule, such as Pax Macedonia, the Roman Empire, and the like, were able to emerge because they offered peace to the people subjugated.
2) Germany now has a one-off lead that it must exploit. Germany mobilized first. Europe understands it needs to unite the continent into a core state to resist Asia and America.
3) Germany and the continent cannot be separated, despite the fixation on "Großdeutschland." Germany needs allies and needs to understand the psychology of Europe.
4) The old European person-centered values are threatened by the degrading Soviet system in which the individual does not count. The Americans threaten Europe from the West. Germany is the outer wall of defense against this.
5) The struggle is not about more prosperity but about spiritual power. The goal is to defend the imperishable values of life and race.
6) The unification of Europe through struggle can only happen when people are won over to support this voluntarily.
7) Our program and goal must be more straightforward than the "Neues Europa" slogan. It must be linked to culture and religion.
8) This European program must be implemented

in the occupied and conquered territories. Since the program is unknown, the attitude of the German occupiers will be leading.
9) German official practice assumes we occupy, but we must be liberators. Human contempt is the hallmark of Bolshevism.
10) Ukraine's current racial exploitation policy creates partisans and is paid for in blood.
11) Europe has been at war for 29 years because of the Slav question. It is essential to resolve that within the idea of the European "Grossraum."[2]
12) Germany had the chance to fight Moscow with the people oppressed by Bolshevism, but we chose the colonialist thesis.
13) We left decisions on the treatment of Eastern European people up to half specialists and lower bars. This did not automatically align with our historical responsibility for the "Grossraumbildung" of our people.
14) Return of land to the people has lagged. Privatization mostly happens in the Baltic states. The looting of the land has contradicted our parole of liberation of the people. Recruitment of labor was more like forced employment.
15) The lack of an extending German policy and the introduction of small sub-interests in the East has led to the distrust of the most promi-

---
2 Oberländer counted from 1914 onward.

nent pro-German people, the Ukrainians. The Ukrainian people wanted to fight with us but were treated and humiliated as helots.
16) Only direct anti-collectivization measures and increased self-government can turn things around. Without help from the Slavs, who make up half the population of Europe, we cannot create a new Europe. The riches of their territory will significantly strengthen Europe.
17) the Slavic people as helot people and inferior. Within Europe, there is no place for colonies anymore.
18) Our problems in the East have three reasons: a) the materialistic racial doctrine, b) the issue of conflict and tension between Deutsche Volksboden and European "Grossraum," and c) Germany is called to play a pioneering role in a new Europe. But in the current power summit, some forces have only had to deal with internal German issues. Their thinking is too narrow and too official.
19) To regain the confidence of the eastern people, the ablest men must be employed, who should serve German interests invisibly.
20) Germany can learn from Japan, which supported self-government among conquered people.
21) Common interest comes before self-interest.

22) Winning over the people of Europe to support our cause is still possible if we have clear goals and treat them well politically.
23) Rome was able to defeat its enemies one by one. Our disadvantage is that we are fighting against the West and the Soviet Union simultaneously. This makes everyone's responsibility all the more significant.
24) Huge opportunities still lie ahead. But action must be taken now, and according to our good rules. We come in the name of the Occident. We can get the support of the nations because our order is unique. By "jeder das seine," we mean that we take into account the people's specific characteristics: unity in diversity.

Oberländer's more rational view on the issue of the Osttruppen remained opposed to that of many Nazi officers and officials regarding Slavic people and Central Asians. Consequently, his role was minimized after January 1943, when the German retreat from the Caucasus began. Oberländer fought against the rigid racial German policy toward the Osttruppen until the end. He also believed that commissars and communists should be spared in order to facilitate the defection of Soviet units. (They were often shot because of the "Kommissarbefehl"). The "Kommissarbefehl" was retracted eventually, but it was too little, too late. Oberländer's flagship unit suffered heavy losses when they retreated from the Caucasus. After the war, in 1968, Oberländer was discredited. This was partly due to a Soviet propaganda offensive in which Oberländer was held responsible for the massacres on the Tama Peninsula, precisely the ones against which he had protested.

Turkmen volunteers

The SS Steals Soldiers from the Army

During that period, a series of acts, instructions, and Denkschriften on how best to deal with the various people emerged. For example, the "Merkblatt für die Behandlung der Tataren" was published on January 9th, 1942, followed by a "Merkblatt" for the Turkmen battalions on June 2nd, 1942. The Einsatzgruppe D, which collaborated with Crimean Tatars, produced a report on February 15th, 1942. On March 20th, the 11th Army wrote the Siefers Report on their experiences with placing Tatar and Caucasian formations within their respective troops. Oskar Ritter von Niedermayer, an expert on Eastern Europe and proficient in Russian, wrote the Grundlegender Befehl about the formation of Turk battalions on July 4th of that year. Someone named Winkler added the report "die politische Lage der Mohammedaner Bosniens" to this on May 4th.

The latter was already pointing toward the division that would later be created, the "13. Waffengebirgsdivision der SS 'Handschar'". There was a lot of thinking and writing about how Nazi Germany could win over the dissatisfied minorities in the

Islamic soldiers serving in the Waffen-SS

Osttruppen at training. Most of them received their training in occupied Poland

Soviet Union. A need was felt to streamline the training of new units, and this was best done in quiet areas behind the front lines. Partly under Niedermayer's influence, an "Ausbildungstab für ausländische Freiwilligen-Verbände" was formed from the "Division Kommando" of the 162nd I.D. This division was moved to Stettin for "auffrischung" on May 18th, 1942.

While the army was in full swing to manage the training and discipline of the Muslim "Ostvölker," officers of the SS suddenly surfaced to look into the matter as well. The army was no longer the only party interested in the Osttruppen. The Reichsführer-SS had set his eyes on the Ostmusel-

Turkmen troops in German service

manischen SS Division and was looking for soldiers. The SS did not hesitate to "cheat" in the process. This soon led to tension between the land forces and the Waffen-SS. One of the first documents found is dated December 11th, 1943, a letter of protest from the army commander of the Turk. Inf.Btl. 790. SS officers came to assess the political attitude and morale of the Turkmen soldiers. The commander firmly rejected this interference, believing the SS had better ask him because "I know the mood here best."

The clash at Turk.battalion 790 was the first in a long line of incidents. On January 5th, 1944, the SS tried to take officers from the Turk.Feld-Btj. I/94. The request came from the Verbindungsstab 1.Muselmansichen SS-Division Neu Turkestan, Berlin Wilmersdorf, Kreuznacherstrasse 12. It went through the Ostministerium (Professor Gerhard von Mende, son of a banker from Riga, professor of economics in Berlin, and professor of Volkstumkunde des Ostraumes) and the General der freiwilligen Verbände via the Chef des Stabes Herre. Two days later, a report came in of soldiers of the Turk. Batl. 786. They were aggressively approached in Warsaw to join the Waffen-SS. Papers were taken from some Turkmen, and they were taken to SS barracks. On January 12th, the Reichsführer-SS himself interfered. He pointed out that Professor Von Mende reported that the Heeresgruppe Süd was working against releasing Islamic units to the Waffen-SS. Himmler asked for help from the Ostministerium to win over the Inspekteur der Osttruppen im OKH, Heinz Hellmich, who was based in the fortified town of Lötzen. Here, he again called on Oberstleutnant Herre, Hellmich's right-hand man. The matter was

Ralph von Heygendorff

to be smoothened through the liaison officers Major Bachmann (OKH/OKW) and Hauptmann Peter (Ostministerium).

All diplomacy and official mediations notwithstanding, the expansion of the Islamic SS units increasingly started to look like a troop raid. On February 14th, the OKH filed a complaint about Mayer-Mader's call for service in the Waffen-SS among Turkmen legionnaires serving in the land forces. This led to the "defection" of 23 soldiers from Turk.Battalion 790. The name of one of them, Tochamanbetow, surfaced in the documents because the OKH knew he was in an SS barrack when the SS denied this. A strange cat-and-mouse game was going on, with one recruiting soldiers from the other and the other reporting these soldiers as deserters, causing military police to search for them. An arrest order went out for a Turk, who was then stationed in Poniatow. In this case, the famous officer Claus Schenk von

Claus Von Stauffenberg, active against the violent recruitment of the SS

Stauffenberg mediated for the army and asked Himmler for clarification.[3]

At the same time, Himmler called on SS-Sturmbannführer Geibel to obtain permission from the OKW to search for Muslim volunteers in various POW camps. After some investigation, it turned out that candidates were indeed found in several camps: Cholm Stalag 319, 182 men; Olchovel Stalag 327, 227 men; Sedlice Stalag 366, 258 men; and reserve Lazarett Petrikau, 57 men.[4]

Von Stauffenberg's complaints were largely ignored, although things did slow down a bit here and there. An investigation on March 2nd, 1944, revealed that SS-Untersturmführer Assankulow had acted too aggressively at the Lager Poniatowa. The following month, SS-Untersturmführer Abdul Dajew showed up at Heeresgruppe Süd to once again recruit among POWs. Dajew carried a pass from the Ostministerium, signed by Professor Von

---

3 According to historian Dossena, Von Stauffenberg was in close contact with Ritter von Niedermayer. He played a crucial role in setting up the legions and became convinced that the war could not be won without help from the Soviet Union. According to his relative Nikolaus von Uxküll-Gyllenband, commander of the Azerbaijani legion, the Osttruppen were "his babies."

4 The whole process was complicated and slow, as usual. In the Nazi bureaucracy, it had to go through many hands. Geibel negotiated with the OKW-authorized General Von Grevenitz and General Wittus in Lublin, commander of the POW system in the Generalgouvernement.

Mende, to support him. On April 11th, Himmler sent his delegates to the northern part of the Eastern Front to search for volunteers in the Baltic region. To this end, Himmler had written to the SS und Polizeiführer (HSSPF) Lithuania in Kauen. The reply came through the "SS-Ersatz-Inspektion Ostland" of the HSSPF Ostland, causing the SS-Hauptamt to complain again about unnecessary delays. On April 26th, 1944, the SS tried to get Crimean Tatars released from the Lager Bietigheim ('Ergänzungsstelle Südwest') near Stuttgart.

DER REICHSFÜHRER-SS
CHEF DES SS-HAUPTAMTES
VS-Nr.   /45 g. -Hr/Ra-
A I - Tgb.Nr.   /45 g.

Berlin-Grunewald, den   16.12.1943
Douglasstraße 7-11

Betr.: Turkmuselmanen-Division

An den
Reichsführer-SS und
Chef der Deutschen Polizei

Berlin SW 11
Prinz-Albrecht-Str. 8

Reichsführer!

1.) Seine Eminenz der Großmufti von Jerusalem wurde am 14.12.1943 mit Major M e i e r - M a d e r und drei seiner turkmenischen Offiziere zusammengebracht. Der Grund des Zusammentreffens war, um die Gelegenheit einer Aussprache zwischen Seiner Eminenz und den turkmenischen Muselmanen wahrzunehmen. Die Unterhaltung dauerte außerordentlich lange und endete mit dem Erfolg, daß es Seiner Eminenz gelungen ist, auch die turkmenischen Offiziere für sich und für den Kampf des Islams gegen die Feindmächte zu begeistern. Die Offiziere gaben Seiner Eminenz einen genauen Bericht über die Lage der muselmanischen Turkvölker. Aufgrund der bisherigen Verwendung der Turkmuselmanen durch das OKW konnten selbstverständlich die turkmenischen Offiziere, aber auch Major M e i e r - M a d e r, ihren Einsatz im Rahmen der SS nur in Form einer legionähnlichen Einheit in der Größe höchstens eines Regiments sehen. Erst nach den Ausführungen Seiner Eminenz erkannten die turkmenischen Offiziere nicht nur die Bedeutung des Einsatzes des gesamten Islam, sondern auch die Erfassung ihrer Stammesgenossen in dem ordentlichen Aufbau einer Division.

-2-

The SS Steals Soldiers from the Army

- 2 -

2.) Bei einer der Mentalität der Turkvölker entsprechenden Behandlung glaube ich, Reichsführer, daß wir mit dem Einsatz dieser Völker im Gesamtrahmen des bisher Erreichten Erfolg haben werden. Die Turkvölker zeichnen sich aus durch ihre große Freiheitsliebe, die auf ihrer starken Religiösität basiert. Diese Freiheitsliebe brachte die Turkvölker auch sofort in einen Gegensatz zum Bolschewismus. Der aktive Kampf der Turkvölker gegen den Bolschewismus dauerte bis 1932. Der Bolschewismus selbst sah ein, daß er die Turkvölker nicht durchdringen konnte und begann, diese auszusiedeln. Diese Aussiedlungsbestrebungen hatten zur Folge, daß ein großer Teil der Turkvölker, besonders die sogenannten Basmatschi (Freischärler) zum Iran, Irak und bis nach China auswichen, so daß also heute große Teile dieser Völkerstämme im Iran und Irak sich befinden.

3.) Auch Seine Eminenz der Großmufti ist der festen Überzeugung, daß, wenn alle bisher erfaßbaren Angehörigen der Turkvölker, die sich bei den Einheiten der Wehrmacht befinden und dort langsam zu Arbeitskompanien umgewandelt werden sollen, zu einer SS-Turkmuselmanen-Division zusammengefaßt werden, der Erfolg nicht ausbleiben und die Auswirkung dieser Zusammenfassung gleich wie bei der Bosniaken-Division auf die muselmanische Welt sehr stark sein wird.

SS-Obergruppenführer

Internal correspondance Reichsführer-SS Himmler regarding the Grossmufti el Hoesseini from Jeruzalem and the deployment of the Osttürks

Professor Gerhard von Mende

From Division to Corps

On May 2nd, 1944, Himmler finally decided that the Ostmuselmanische unit, often considered a regiment, should be given divisional status. As a result, even the prisoner-of-war camps in Norway were searched for usable men. On May 5th, an urgent request was made to send propaganda material from Dabendorf, Berlin. Via a Lufthansa transport, this was hastily brought in. On May 8th, SS-Obersturmbannführer Nasarow searched Unit I/94 again thoroughly. This unit was filled with wounded men recovering, so there were new men in the unit each time. On the 22nd of that month, the SS in Bucharest took over a unit of Crimean Tatars for the Waffen-SS from Alfred Erdmann of the Ostministerium. The SS Hauptamt was very enthusiastic, as was shown by the order that followed on June 7th, 1944, to turn the Ostmuselmanischen Division into a real army corps.

The Grossmufti of Jerusalem, El-Hoesseini, was deployed to improve the relationship between Germany and Muslims. Mayer-Mader, who was now "hired" by the SS, hooked up with the "eminence" on December 14th, 1943, accompanied by three Turkmen officers. El-Hoesseini supported the Nazi struggle against Judaism, had visited Auschwitz, and had given his approval to recruit Bosnian Muslims for the "Handschar" division and other Islamic Waffen-SS units. He was deeply anti-Jewish and had urged the German Luftwaffe and Hermann Göring on several occasions in 1943 and 1944 to bomb "Jewish targets" in Palestine (Tel Aviv) to make a "statement" in the Arab world. German secret sabotage missions in Palestine, where they were dropped by parachute, were carried out in part by men selected by El-Hoesseini. The October 1944 drop is an example of this. It was commanded by Lieutenant Kurt Wieland, a Palestinian German and former member of the "Brandenburg" unit. He went via Athens and jumped with his men above Jericho. Vigilant British troops, however, quickly managed to intercept them. The German press widely used his visit to the Bosnian Waffen-SS division "Handschar" to show that Berlin was serious about their alliance with Islam. The idea behind it was that they were fighting the same enemies, "international Jewry" and the Western colonial powers, who were oppressing the Arabs. At the time, no independent Islamic state existed outside of Turkey.

The Grossmufti spoke words to Mayer-Mader's heart when he stated that not only an SS regiment but Islam as a whole needed to be mobilized. Mayer-Mader noted in his report after the conversation that he believed military cooperation could be very successful if religiosity and love of freedom among the Turk people and other Muslim volunteers were given the right consideration. He pointed out that the Turkmen had resisted communism as late as 1932. It was also decided an imam institute in Berlin would be established under the auspices of the Grossmufti.

These ideas were endorsed by Emil Hermann, who also dealt with Muslim SS volunteers. He argued that the "Basmatschi," the resistance fighters against Bolshevism, lived among the Turks. According to him, their militancy stemmed from the fact that the Turkmen had not been under as much foreign influence as the Arabs. As a result, Bolshevism had "hardly penetrated" the Turkmen, Kyrgyz, Tajiks, Uzbeks, and Azerbaijanis, making them even more freedom-oriented.

Decoration for Azerbaijani soldier

Mayer-Mader vs. Hermann, Goals and Ambitions Concerning the Osttruppen

Mayer-Mader and Hermann shared these insights, but there were also issues within the SS regarding direction and course on which they disagreed. Hermann warned the Reichsführer-SS about the somewhat hazy nature of Mayer-Mader's actions. He justifiably stated that Mayer-Mader had hardly gotten around to building an actual unit, even though there were at least 30,000 Turkmen "volunteers" within the prison camps, construction battalions, and other units. In contrast, Mayer-Mader was taken by the idea of igniting an Islamic insurgency on the southeastern flank of the Soviet Union. Thus Mayer-Mader was setting up a provisional government of Turkmenistan. He was building support bases in Iraq, Iran, and Azerbaijan, uniting freedom fighters (the Basmatschi) for an intervention of the diaspora Turkmen towards the Soviet Union. Hermann stated that, in doing so, Mayer-Mader followed the line of "Schellenberg" (and Oberländer to some extent). He also immediately concluded that they were aiming too high. There was no capacity to realize such lofty

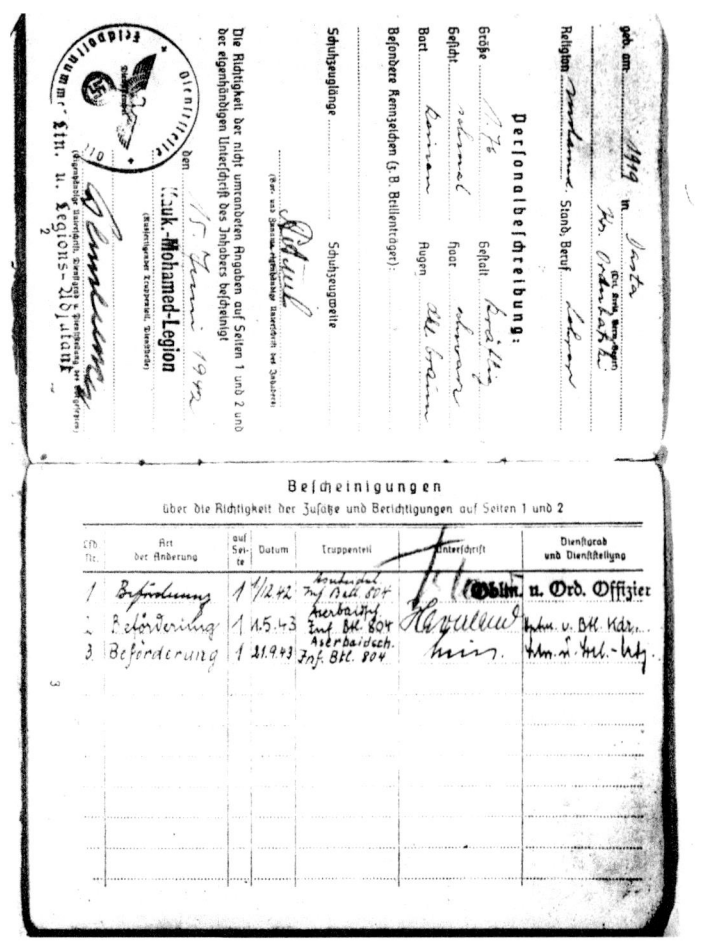

Soldbuch

plans. According to Hermann, this was only possible if the Grossmufti was involved. On top of that, there was not only a great need for ideas but also for a "festes Instrument," a division. It was precisely that which Mayer-Mader failed to organize. Hermann experienced it all firsthand and was in touch with the needs of his Turkmen troops, men who would make up the bulk of the new division. Thus, on December 15th, Hermann informed Himmler that the soldiers needed a flag to symbolize their unit. This flag was drawn up and described as consisting of different colored stripes, each representing a Turkmen tribe, which came together in the crescent of Islam. The color green prevailed, of course, as the color of Islam.

These internal memos from Hermann to Himmler were probably partly the cause of the later downfall of Mayer-Mader. It eventually propelled Hermann to become the temporary commander of the "Neu Turkestan" unit. Both men would not outlive their momentum for long.

Unaware of the card game going on above their heads, "benevolent" Germans tried to make the men comfortable. Preserved documents from the Ostmuselmanischen unit mention the arrival of a guitar, a mandolin, harmonicas, and five chess sets. Fifty German translations of the Koran were ordered from Reklam Verlag for the German staff. According to documents dated April 7th, 1944, the bill went to the SS-Hauptamt. On April 27th, the head of the SS-Hauptamt, Gottlob Berger, provided five thousand cigarettes and five watches to be

> **IM NAMEN DES FUHRERS**
>
> IST DEM
>
> J a r a s c h o w , Sadulla
>
> Aserb.Inf.Btl. 804
>
> **AM** 22.6.1943
>
> DIE
>
> **VERDIENST-AUSZEICHNUNG FÜR ANGEHÖRIGE DER OSTVÖLKER 2. KLASSE IN BRONZE**
> **VERLIEHEN WORDEN.**
>
> Der Befehlshaber Krim
> I. V.
> *[signature]*
> Generalleutnant

Decoration Azerbaijani volunteer

given to officers, good soldiers of the Ostmuselmanischen SS.⁵

Now that they had the go-ahead from the authority of Husseini, the SS-Hauptamt, and the Reichsführer-SS, Mayer-Mader could get to work. The HSSPF Lublin, SS-Gruppenführer Jakob Sporrenberg, was asked to help set up the new SS unit. He was instructed to "not bureaucratically disrupt this process." The SS officer of the Hauptamt, Gerd Schulte, was well informed about the "Paper Wars" that regularly arose within the German offices. Space became available in the Lager Poniatowa near Lublin to assemble and train a few thousand men. They later moved to Juraciszki near Minsk. Sporrenberg was an older Nazi and had been with the right-wing camp since the Kapp-Putsch. He spent two years in French prisons because of his opposition to the Ruhr occupation. He was Odilo Globocknik's successor, who had long held power in this part of occupied Poland and had pursued a sheer extermination policy against the Jews.

On January 13th, 1944, the SS-Hauptamt reaf-

---

5 For the map department, exotic maps of Damascus, Cairo, lower Egypt, Morocco, Tunisia, Turkey, and India were provided. In the SS, lots were still daydreaming, although fewer and fewer shared this dream. On February 21st, the suicide of a German cadre soldier, Herman Schaechter, was reported. Under the influence of alcohol, he shot himself in the head. On the way to the infirmary, partisans shot at the transport.

firmed the need for the new division. Mayer-Mader was officially appointed as the division's drafter. He was to be succeeded later by career SS officer Emiel Hermann. To keep the various lines of communication open, a "Verbindungsstab" was established in Berlin at Neue Douglasstrasse 11. The liaison officer was SS-Hauptsturmführer Schmidtberger. Mayer-Mader arrived in Cracow on January 15th, and with the support of various agencies, the build-up began.

Three battalions were formed; the I. battalion under SS-Untersturmführer Asankulow, a Kirgian, the II. battalion under SS-Obersturmführer Fürst, and the III. battalion under Hauptsturmführer Alekberliew, an Azerbaijani. In the official records, the unit was now an Ostmuselmanischen SS-Division, 1. Regiment, address Poniatowa, Post Opole, Kreis Pulaway, District of Lublin. The site was accessible by railroad up to Maleczow, then by small tracks, and through the partisan territory, to Rosalino, after which it was five kilometers on foot to Poniatowa. On January 21st, 1944, internal reports still did not favor the unit. It was believed to be "a collection of soldiers, lacking all connection," and there were "too few German executives."

The number of men grew slowly. They were still waiting for all sorts of transport. The picture was as follows: mostly Turkmen, except for Azerbaijanis in

Cigarettes and watches for the volunteers

the I. and III. battalions. The unit had about 3,000 men by the end of the month. A third of those men were still serving in the Red Army a few months earlier and did not even have German uniforms.

Hermann had assembled a small team of German officers and non-commissioned officers; Mayer-Mader as commander, Fürst (from the SD/Abwehr), Bünger, Kupa, Gutermuth (interpreter), Suleiman (interpreter), and Kortas as foreman.

While the unit was literally "in the middle of nowhere," Mayer-Mader was always on the move. Of course, there was a good reason for that. He wanted to build up and gather troops. But it was out of balance with his fieldwork, which had already been a problem in the army. On January 26th, Himmler seriously reprimanded him because of reports of the messy situation at the "Neu Turkestan" unit. According to Himmler, the unit was becoming increasingly "Turkmen," and German officers were hardly ever greeted. There was a culture of disobedience; people were not listening. A Kyrgyz officer, Asankulow, went to the ss-Hauptamt on his own to ask where the SS collar mirrors remained, which did not land well in Berlin. They did not appreciate receiving orders from a Kyrgyz volunteer! Everything was in the hands of Turkmen and Azerbaijanis, who had been appointed officers by Mayer-Mader without restraint. The fact that Mamed Sulejmanow, an ss-Obersturmführer, was deputy regimental commander was too much to handle. Mayer-Mader was summoned to the ss-Hauptamt.

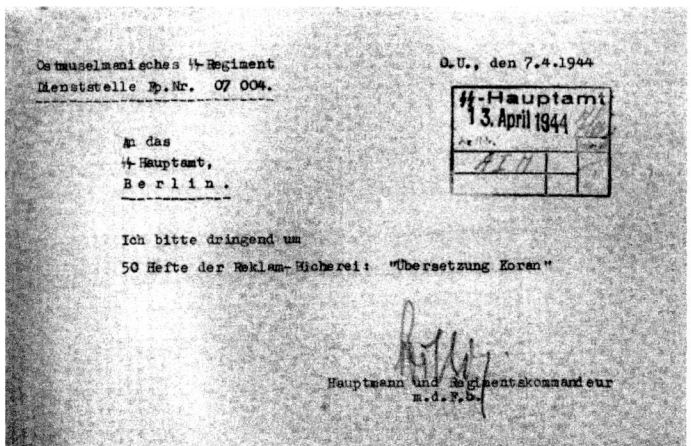

Purchase of fifty Korans by the SS-Hauptamt

For Andreas Mayer-Mader, this was the beginning of the end. His ultimate fate is still uncertain, but he was likely demoted in rank. After legal proceedings against him (which included the complaint that he called army soldiers to defect to the SS), he was probably assigned to the infamous SS Brigade "Dirlewanger," where he is said to have died on May 2nd, 1944.

Stationing of the SS-Sondertruppe december 1944

Trouble in Polish Trawniki

The issues around discipline worsened within the Ostmuselmanischen unit. Things got out of hand in late January and early February between Polish workers stationed nearby and the Muslim SS volunteers. The Poles were in the SS training camp Trawniki (Block 19) near Poniatowa. Surveillance teams from 11./Pol. Rgt. 25 and the "Kommando Poniatowa" kept this camp separated from the SS men. But there was less surveillance at the time because of a "Judenaktion."

SS soldiers penetrated the homes of the Poles. Several reports mentioned trespassing. Turkmen forced themselves on Polish women, scolded them for being "Jewess," and went after the daughters (aged thirteen). Polish workers and sentinels rushed in, intervened, and prevented worse things from happening. In nearby Naleczow, a series of incidents occurred.

A Polish smuggler was "spared" from arrest in exchange for sex and robbed by a Turkmen. Two other Turkmen attempted to rape a Polish woman, Wilko-Laska. She had "bite marks" on her body and was told they would "shoot and kill" her if reported. Maria Milnik, a 13-year-old girl, was assaulted.

Transfer to Minsk and Juraciszki

In the meantime, they tried to expand the unit further. The Turk battalion 450 was one of the first larger units Hermann and Mayer-Mader tried to take over and add to the Ostmuselmanischen unit. After a long tug-of-war, the battalion, commanded by Hauptmann Kob, was placed under the authority of the Waffen-SS on December 18th, 1943. New problems arose. Transporting the unit proved to be a major issue. Once again, a "Paper War" was waged, this time about the agencies of the HSSPF Russland Mitte and Weisruthenien and the OKH. Most importantly, the battalion was not assigned train transportation. On March 2nd, 1944, it got stuck in Balownaja, twelve kilometers north of Nikolayev. Meanwhile, the Ostmuselmanischen unit had moved from Poniatowa to Juraciszkibee, near Minsk. Trains were supposed to go from Odessa to the hinterland, but the route was clogged entirely by the great retreat underway. SS-Oberscharführer Keuschel was sent to the "Transportkommandotur" to insist that the battalion be considered urgent. Keuschel reported to the head of the SS-Hauptamt Gottlob Berger, who threatened to inform the Reichsführer-SS if the "Transportkommandotur" delayed any longer. But the power of the SS was more limited than we might think. The army's transport chief kept his cool. On March 30th, 1944, he decided the lone Turk battalion was not more important than the escape of all those German units moving westward from Odessa. The best alternative was to march to Braila to find another rail connection.

The Terror of Heinz Billig and the Desertion of Asangulow

At the beginning of 1943, the first units from Poniatowa slowly started coming into Juraciszki near Minsk. The Turkmen were stationed in Juraciszki and the Azerbaijanis in Kosti. Unfortunately, without Mayer-Mader, the command was put into the hands of SS-Hauptsturmführer Heinz Billig. Today, Billig would probably be considered a traumatized officer, for he took everything out on his soldiers. Executions of Osttruppen happened on a daily basis. Billig knew only of the stick and used it for the slightest offenses. The commander was an alcoholic, and that turned out disastrously. When he was doing a tour to inspect the sentinels, he asked a Turkman for the password. When the Turkmen told him the password had not been reported to him yet, Billig threw a hand grenade at him. He made dozens of soldiers shoot their fellow soldiers; the Turkmen shot the Azerbaijanis and vice versa. This created bad blood between the two camps. He overplayed his hand when one of the most prominent volunteers,

SS-Unterscharführer Agaew, requested a transfer after a conflict. He had him executed for "disobedience."

The response was inevitable. Forty-eight men of the 2nd Company, commanded by SS-Untersturmführer Asangulow, defected to the partisans. Among those troops were three more officers. At the time, Asangulow was a part of Mayer-Mader's "Vorkommando." It didn't stop there. On April 2nd, partisans attacked Juraciszki's training center. They tried to get the entire unit to join the partisans' side. This did not happen, but about 100 men did desert. All sorts of rumors were going around in the camp, partly spread by the Communists, who claimed that Mayer-Mader was, in fact, a Russian spy. On April 24th, another ten men deserted and took everything they had with them, including their weapons.

Neu Turkestan and the Infamous Brigade "Dirlewanger"

Enough was enough for the HSSPF Von Gottberg, who controlled the area behind the front lines around Minsk. He decided to place the messy and undisciplined unit under the command of the "Dirlewanger" unit immediately. Billig was removed from his post due to drunkenness but also because of a homosexuality charge. On April 6th, SS-Hauptsturmführer Emil Hermann took office as the new commander. Hermann's arrival was a blessing, as the men had been treated like "cattle" until then. Promises were made to open a brothel for the soldiers to improve the general mood. Twenty-five Tatar girls were to be brought in for the officers. In Vienna, they were also organizing the 1st "Kongress National-Turkestanischen Einheitskommitees," to be held from June 8th to June 10th, 1944. Hermann, SS-Haupsturmführer Alimow, and SS-Untersturmführer Kamalow of the unit were to participate. This way, the Germans wanted to show they were serious about self-determination. On May 30th, 1944, another 487 Crimean Tatars left Vienna Station to join the unit. Among them was the clergyman Asisow Abdul Karim. At the same time, reinforcements from the Turk Battalion 450 finally arrived, compensating for the losses caused by desertion. This was essential because only 800 men had been transferred to the "Sonderbrigade Dirlewanger" under Hermann, as we know from a message from "Dirlewanger" dated May 20th, 1944. There was, however, the prospect of another 600 men coming from Norway who had been successfully recruited from POW camps. Hermann retained his post only until May 2nd, 1944, probably due to the unit's reassignment to "Dirlewanger." On July 11th, 1944, Hermann was killed in an anti-Partisan action. As a result, he did not participate in the Vienna Congress.

This also meant the Ostmuselmanische SS men were now under the command of one of the most controversial SS officers. Dirlewanger's unit had developed a ruthless reputation in the anti-partisan struggle. Its core was made up of poachers from all the prisons of Europe. The "romantic" Himmler believed these "natural men" would make good soldiers in the partisan's forest areas. In addition, the division was created out of penal military units and "antisocials." Also, they had some experience with Osttruppen. A document dated June 8th, 1943, states that 760 "Russians" served in the unit, including Ukrainians. The largest units of these were three companies, each including 150 Russians. Wherever the "Dirlewanger" unit appeared, enemy resistance ceased to exist, but so did life. That was pretty much the motto of the unit that used the crossed steel hand grenades and carbines as a symbol. The unit's losses were enormous.[6] Himmler himself characterized the culture within the unit as "medieval." At a meeting with Nazi notables in Posen, he let slip that if you looked at someone the wrong way or doubted final victory, you were soon "dead on the ground." He added: "There is no other way to lead such a unit." Dr. Oskar Dirlewanger, the commander, had been penalized (for sexual offenses with underage girls) but had always remained out of harm's way due to his good relationship with his old comrade Berger of the SS-Hauptamt. This would remain so even after the unit's serious misconduct during the crushing of the Warsaw Uprising. Because of his petite stature, Dirlewanger's nickname was Gandhi, but he could not have been further away from pacifism.

---

6 An article in the Vopersal archive reported that the losses of "Dirlewanger" were about 100% every quarter. This was probably an exaggeration, but it does indicate that human life was not worth much at "Dirlewanger." The author owns a copy of this article.

Dr. Oskar Dirlewanger

Warsaw

There was not much time for training the Osttruppen. "Dirlewanger" and the Osttruppen were swept westward when they rapidly retreated toward Bialystok due to the Soviet offensive. While the unit was retreating, recruitment for the "division" continued unabated in Lublin, Warsaw, and other major cities in the German occupation zone. Men from the Arbeitseinsatz were also lured into the division. A new build-up period was provided for the unit, first in Usda, later in Hungary, near Kaposvar. In Minsk, the men were deloused before the trip continued.[7] After Hermann's death, SS-Sturmbannführer Franz Liebermann took charge of the unit in late July or early August 1944. Meanwhile, in Poniatowa ("Aufgangslager Poniatowa"), men continued to be gathered for the unit. Ernst Friedrich Christoph (Fritz) Sauckel was requested to send men serving in the Arbeitseinsatz, causing 220 Crimean Tatars to be marched to the "Auffanglager" on May 12th, 1944. Three days lat-

---
7 T 354 Roll 651 Der Höhere SS und Polizeiführer Russland Mitte und Weissruthenien St.Qu. dem 1 Mai 1944.

Islamic soldiers serving in the Waffen-SS

Revolt in Warsaw

er, troops were released from the Ostarbeiterlager Strasshof, about 550 men.

While the units were preparing for transport to Hungary, the Warsaw Uprising broke out in Poland. Brigade "Dirlewanger" became highly notorious there. The unit arrived at the outskirts of Warsaw on August 2nd, 1944. They murdered and behaved erratically and unruly. Even Von dem Bach Zelewski, an SS heavyweight, could hardly get a grip on the unique manner in which Dirlewanger led his unit. Upon the conquest of an illegal liquor distillery, the march stopped entirely. SS officers were threatened upon inspection.

As a person, Dirlewanger was a fearless man and of unprecedented audacity. Falsely reporting to the top was second nature to him. But he was also hard on himself, was wounded no less than 11 times, and was eventually murdered by former prisoners after the war. Due to his close ties with Berger, he was awarded the "Ritterkreuz" on September 30th, 1944, for his efforts in Warsaw. Von dem Bach Zelewski was not so convinced about the qualities of this unit. He repeatedly asked the OKW for regular infantry and additional ammunition. "We just can't kill them all," his right-hand man Heinz Reinefarth complained.

Which units went into action exactly in Warsaw remains unclear. Even Von dem Bach Zelewski spoke of a "mishmash" of units, which his chief of staff, SS-Gruppenführer Reinefarth, had to operate. Norman Davies' established work on the Warsaw Uprising does not clarify this entirely. In any case, the SS brigade of SS-Brigadeführer Mechislav Kamiński was mentioned. It fell under the General der Freiwilligenverbände General Köstring and was about 2,000 men strong. The SS-Brigade "Dirlewanger" was mentioned as well (3,381 men, including the Azerbaijani battalion 111, two Cossack battalions (572 and 580)), and a combat unit commanded by Willy Schmidt from Breslau, police units, Luftwaffe guard units, and a reserve battalion of the Hermann Göring armored paratroopers. A surviving document from the Heeresgruppe Mitte

Dirlewanger in Warsaw

of the 9th Army, dated October 3rd, 1944, reports a series of other small units. The document also led to some corrections:

Infantry:
Sich.Rgt. 608 with I. and II. battalion
Sich.Btl. 350
Lds.Schtz.Btle. 246, 996, 997, and 998
Artillery:
Karl-Bttr. 428
SS.Stellungs-Werf.Bttr-, 201

Panzer:
Pz.Abt. 302
Sturm Pz.Kp. 218
Sturm Ers.Kp. 1000
Eisenbahn Panzer-Lehrzug 5
Pioneering:
Pi.Btle. 46 and 627
Sturm Pi.Btl. 500
Sturm Pi.Btl. 501
Horch und Minierzug Kp. 7
Pi.Bohr-Zug
Pi.Bau-Btl. 737

Freiwillige Verbände:
Kos.Btl. 527
Kos.Reiter-Abt. 580
IV./(Kos.)Sich.Rgt. 57
Kos.Abt. 69
3./Kos. Rgt
I./Aserb. 111
II./Aserb. Bergmann

The above list reported the "Splittereinheiten" that fought in Warsaw. The divisions were not mentioned, but in the immediate vicinity, the 25th Pz.D., Kampfgruppe "Bernhard" (Korück 532) and the 1st Luftwaffe Felddivision, larger units, still operated. From this list, it can be deduced that the

Ostmuselmanische Osttruppen most likely operated within the "Dirlewanger" unit. In any case, they were not included in this list of small units. It also cannot be ruled out completely that the volunteers served in the SS-Pol (Polizei) Schtz.Rgt. 34, which had 33 officers and 651 men. However, this included 982 "Freiwilligen" with no further specification.

Participation in Osttruppen during the crushing of the Warsaw Uprising happened on a much larger scale than Davies listed. This concerns the Cossacks, but more importantly for our research, the two Azerbaijani units, the I.battalion of the Azerbaijani regiment 111 and a battalion of Bergmann (II. Aserb.Bergmann). The I.battalion is often misrepresented as a regiment. It was a battalion of the 111th regiment, which initially belonged to the 111th I.D., and later to the Heeresgruppe as part of the Azerbaijani legion. According to military historian Georg Tessin, the battalion was established in the winter of 1942-1943. Both units were not part of the Waffen-SS. They were certainly not part of the Ostmuselmanische unit, given that the October 3rd report did not include SS units. However, they probably did operate temporarily within the ranks of "Dirlewanger" or "Kaminski." According to historian Philip W. Blood, two battalions of "Eastern Muslims" were under the command of "Dirlewanger" on October 5th. The two Azerbaijani units were mentioned separately, so they probably served in the ranks of Kaminski, both as part of the Korpsgruppe Von dem Bach Zelewski and within that Korpsgruppe in the Kampfgruppe Reinefarth. That group, together with the Kampfgruppe Rohr, stopped the attack.

It seems that most of the Ostmuselmanischen unit arrived in Warsaw late in the battle. The historians Böhler and Gewarth wrote that "Dirlewanger" requested reinforcements of the "Neu Turkestan" on August 9th but that this unit had already accidentally been sent towards Hungary by the railroads. This caused a delay, so the men did not arrive until August 14th, 1944.

Orders coming from Himmler himself caused the excessive use of violence. He was supposedly furious about the Warsaw uprising. He wanted to show Europe what it would mean to rebel against Germany. The massacre was enormous, especially in the Wola district. "We fought for Warsaw for five weeks," Himmler stated, looking back. "It was the hardest battle we have fought." The Poles paid a terrible price. For every German killed, twenty Poles perished. The Polish were defeated because they were cut off from supply and resupply, but also because of a divided resistance, which, according to German reports, also shot at each other on several occasions. In this case, the Polish national-minded resistance was at odds with the communist-inspired resistance. Support operations coming from outside Warsaw, such as from the south near the Kampinos Forest (Kamopinoska), were pushed back. The Chojnowskie forest area south of Warsaw and the forest area between Tomaszow and Betrikau were also unsettled. The Germans executed Kaminksi and his right-hand man Ilya Stavikin for their misbehavior and the anarchy within their unit. Kaminski defended the looting of his troops, stating that his people had "lost everything." He was executed, but his men were told Polish rebels had killed him. Kaminski and Dirlewanger fought side by side within

Unit logo 'Turkistan'

Kampfgruppe Von Gottberg against partisans during operation "Frühlingsfest" in the spring of 1944 in Belarus. Barely a year and a half later, Kaminski was executed, and Dirlewanger was allowed to join a dinner with Von dem Bach Zelewski in honor of his "Ritterkreuz."

The role of "Neu Turkestan" in Warsaw remains obscure. In any case, troops were deployed there in a later phase, as there are loss lists of German officials killed. This involved just over 200 men killed and wounded. This leads to the conclusion that there was severe fighting going on. In total, "Neu Turkestan" lost 14 officers, and 53 non-commissioned officers were killed and wounded in the battle for Warsaw. The unit "Dirlewanger" also suffered considerable losses. The exact numbers have not been found, but historians Mallmann and Paul spoke of "hundreds of men lost." The historian Paolo A. Dossena noted that the worst massacres caused by the Islamic forces in the Wola district involved mainly the two Azerbaijani units.

Harun el-Raschid Bey and the Slovak Uprising

When the cannons went silent in Warsaw on October 2nd, the expansion of the Ostmuselmanischen unit was resumed. In a memo dated October 20th, 1944, Himmler spoke of the Ostturkischen Waffenverband der SS, showing that he had not yet given up on his dreams of larger units. A new commander was also appointed. After a short interim period (September-October 1944) under Reiner Olzscha, a medic specialized in Central Asian diseases and attached to the University of Berlin, SS-Standartenführer Harun el-Raschid Bey, was put forward. His birth name was Wilhelm Hintersatz. In him, the SS had once again found a man who, like Mayer-Mader, had his heart set on Islam and had an eye for the possibilities of exploiting it militarily and politically. Hintersatz was from Brandenburg and served in Turkey in World War I under Otto Linman von Sanders, a German general who tried to reform the Turkish army to align with Western standards. Hintersatz got involved in intelligence work after World War I, dealing with former Islamic prisoners of war. He had also done

Slovak freedom fighters taking action against Nazi-Germany

intelligence work for the Italians in Abyssinia. Based on these experiences, he had a certain authority regarding knowledge of Islam. The Muslims saw a fellow believer in him, which strengthened his position. Under his Islamic name Harun el-Raschid Bey, they would expand further into Slovakia. Together with the Brigade "Dirlewanger," the unit was transported and arrived in Rosenberg, Slovakia, on October 12th, 1944. A new Imam, Nureddin Namangani, had also been appointed to the troops and was given the rank of SS-Untersturmführer.

The troops arrived in a burned-down country. In August 1944, a national uprising broke out under Jan Golian against the fascist-clerical regime of Joseph Tiso. However, due to uncoordinated actions and premature violence, the German army and SS

German troops enter Gottschee (Kocerje), Slovkia 1944

units were able to put down the insurgent army successfully. The focus of the fighting was in central Slovakia. On October 17th, the German command in the region, under General Hermann Höfle, situated in Pressburg (Bratislava), ensured units were ready to put down the Slovak uprising. Just like in Warsaw, the occupying forces of the occupied territories consisted of weaker units and splinter groups. Units were rushed in, including "Dirlewanger," to reinforce the operation. They needed to hurry, as military intelligence predicted that on November 20th, the Red Army would be able to physically contact the approximately 24,000 Slovak insurgents. Additionally, the Slovak troops cut off the return route of the German forces. In many ways, therefore, the Slovak uprising was even more dangerous for Germany than the one in Warsaw, even though not much historical attention has been paid to the matter.

Höfle, an Austrian in the circle of SS'ers around SS commander Odilo Globocnik and involved in the Holocaust (in operation "Reinhardt" and the deportations from the Warsaw Ghetto), envisioned a short, solid eleven-day campaign. To this end, he brought several units in, including the "Tatra" division, Kampfgruppe "Schill," the 18th SS division "Horst Wessel," a Kampfgruppe consisting of former soldiers from the 14th (Ukrainian) SS "Galizien" division (Kampfgruppe "Wittenmeyer"), and the newly arrived "Dirlewanger" and "Neu Turkestan." "Dirlewanger," commanded by Walter Schi-

Slovak Partisans flee into the mountains

The Red Army reaches the Slovakian border

mana at the time, was fighting on the northern front. The Slovaks drew the short straw. About 10,000 men fled into the mountains to join the partisans. Others went into hiding in civilian society. "Burning vehicles were seen everywhere on the mountain roads. Nothing was allowed to fall into the hands of enemies. It was a sad sight," recalled one Slovak insurgent later. Banska Bystrica, the center of the Slovak uprising, had fallen. Tiso held a victory parade. The Red Army would not be in town until March 26th.

"Dirlewanger" was 5,500 troops strong during the operation, probably including Neu Turkestan. The unit fought in a tough front line. There were excellent bunkers and positions in the valleys around the mountains, leaving the German troops with little freedom to move. They tried in vain to advance southward to Banska Bystrica from Rosenberg several times. Eventually, the Slovaks kept 12 by 12 kilometers at Liptovska Osada, Korytnica, Kaliste, Donovaly, and Stare Hory. In cooperation with Kampfgruppe Schill and units of "Horst Wessel," these were eventually destroyed. In total, more than 4,000 Slovak insurgents died.

Slovakian rebels

Downfall in Lombardy

When the crisis in Slovakia was over, new tasks were already waiting for the special units. By October 1944, things had also started to shift in Hungary. This ally tried to switch to the Allied side, and Von dem Bach Zelewski had the castle in Buda stormed and the son of the Reich Regent Miklos Horthy arrested. This muted the defection and helped the arrow-crossing fascists of Ferenc Szálasi come into power.

On Christmas night, 1944, Budapest was surrounded by the Red Army. The final phase of the war began. In January, the Heeresgruppe Süd desperately fought during the «Konrad» operations to free the 72,000 men in the Budapest garrison. In March 1945, during operation «Frühlingserwachen,» they attempted to push back the Red Army across the Danube and onto the oil fields of Romanian Ploesti. The commander of the 6th SS-Pz. Army, Joseph (Sepp) Dietrich, wanted to give these fields to Hitler as a birthday gift. The plans were unrealistic, despite the reinforcements brought to the east after the failure of the Ardennes Offensive.

"Neu Turkestan" was on Slovak soil for a long time, although they were drawn into the Red Army's Hungarian operations eventually. On November 2nd, the unit lined up once again. It was under the jurisdiction of the HSSPF Slovakia, SS-Obergruppenführer Hermann Höfle. The battalions were scaled up again based on ethnicity: I. Turkestan, II. Tatars from the Idel-Ural region and III. the Azerbaijani battalion. Eventually, the size was between 6,000 and 8,000 troops. The scrambling for troops continued, and the scarcity of officers persisted. For example, officer Gerd Schulte of the Albanian SS unit "Skanderbeg" was transferred to "Neu Turkestan." In December 1944, new Crimean Tatar troops joined the unit.

But the constantly receding front lines and the uncertain future of the "free Caucasian republics," as well as the ever-difficult cooperation between the Germans and the Osttruppen, led to another major desertion on December 25th, 1944, during Christmas. After a conflict with SS-Hauptsturmführer Fürst, several hundred volunteers went on the run, led by Ghulam Alimow, and deserted in the vicinity of Nove Mesto, where they hid in the woods. An attempt to bring in the Azeris, under the command of Abdul Fatalibey, failed. German officers were even shot at. An SS-Unterscharführer immediately alerted Harun el-Raschid Bey, who had pamphlets scattered over the forests calling on the deserted soldiers to return. He promised to waive criminal charges. Alimov still refused to return and hid in the village of Propat. However, around 200 to 300 men chose to play it safe and returned to the Germans in Nove Mesto.

Just as after every setback, the Germans regrouped. It is unclear whether Harun el-Raschid Bey remained in command. Either way, as of December 15th, documents spoke of the Osttürkischer Waffen-Verband der SS, set up in Miawa, Slovakia. Azerbaijani troops were removed from the unit and transferred to the Caucasian Waffen-Verband der SS. The latter units were moved to northern Italy for further deployment. In exchange for the Azerbaijanis, in January 1945, the Waffen-Gebirgs-Brigade ("Tatarian" No. 1) was assigned to the Ostmuselmanian unit. This unit was led at the "Kurmark" military training grounds. After all the restructuring was completed, the unit was more or less at the division level. It had three regiments, each with two battalions, eight companies, and two heavyweight companies. The "regiments" were referred to as "SS-Waffengruppe" and were named "Turkestan," "Crimea," and "Iden Ural." By February 1945, the number of soldiers in the unit had reached 8,500. In a document probably dating from the spring of 1945, the Osttürkischer Waffen-Verband der SS also still bears the name "Timur," and the "Caucasian Waffen-Verband der SS" bears the name "Schamil," both named after Islamic field commanders. The unit now appeared on the Lagekarte of Heeresgruppe Süd as Osttürkischen Waffen-Verband der SS "Harun el-Raschid." At least until March and possibly longer, it remained in the hinterland of the 8th Army in Slovakia. The unit was also temporarily assigned to the 48th I.D., thus becoming part of the 8th Army again. It usually still fell under the "Deutsche Befehlshaber in der Slowakei" Höfle. By January 1945, the unit was separated, at least physically, from "Dirlewanger," which was located in Priewitz (Prievidzo). Parts of the unit, a battalion and an artillery battery, had been temporarily deployed with the 24th Pz.D. (Anlage KTB Hgr Süd 30-12-1944). The «Dirlewanger" unit still received divisional status in February 1945. The other Slovak battle units, such as "Tatra" and "Schill," were stationed more to the south, near Sered (Lagekart 12-01-1945, Anlage KTB Hgr.Süd).

In late March or early April, the unit surfaced in Italy, around Mailand in Lombardy, where most of them stayed. Some of the Turkestan troops were still deployed near Carpi, in the province of Modena. The HSSPF Karl Wolff quantified their strength as 3,800 troops. In a document prepared by the

Downfall in Lombardy

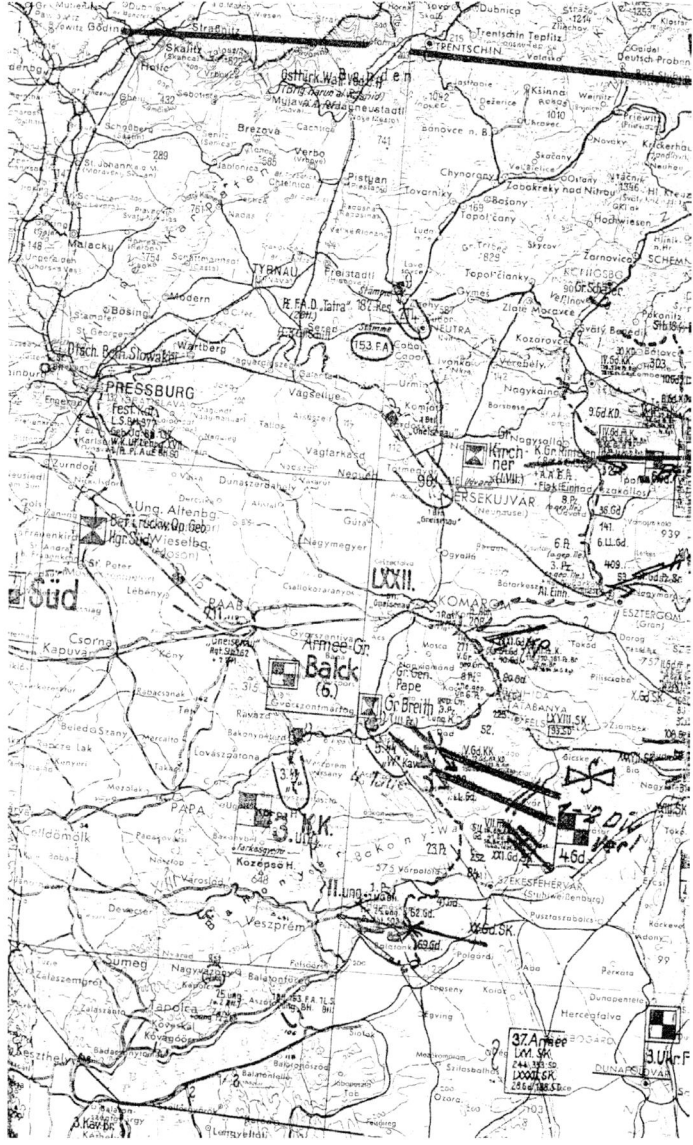

Hungarian front 1945. The Osttürkische unit was active due north of Pressbug (Bratislava)

"Georgian Komitee" in Berlin on March 26th, 1945, which stubbornly insisted on fighting Bolshevism, the number of Osttruppen in German service at that time was said to be 102,295 troops. Most were in 41 field battalions, the 314th Azerbaijani Infantry Regiment (162nd I.D.), the legions (48,700 men), the construction battalions (21,595 men), within German units (25,000 men), in the Waffen-SS, SS, SD, and Luftwaffe (7,000 men). The men of "Neu Turkestan" fell into this last group.

The arrival of Islamic volunteers on Italian territory was not new. Earlier, 24 Ost battalions had found their way to Italy. The 162nd (Turk) I.D. was also moved from the Neuhammer training grounds to Italy in August/September 1943. Many Osttruppen (including the Cossacks) had also served in the part of the Balkans occupied by Italians.

The new assignment of "Harun el-Raschid" was to occupy, secure and combat partisans, but it was obvious to all that the end of the war was near. Once again, desertion occurred. Some defections were prevented and limited by police units. Around 150 men deserting were reportedly killed near Col di Nesse. Hintersatz did not see his troops as a Napoleonic guard who would fight to their death, so on April 26th, 1945, he consulted with the partisans in his region. He wanted to sit out the war without further bloodshed. A treaty was drawn up in which they agreed that the troops would await the arrival of the Americans in the barracks at Merate. On April 30th, the Americans captivated the remnants of the "Neu Turkestan" unit. Little is known about their fate after that, but these Osttruppen were mostly extradited to the Soviet Union, where death surely awaited them. Before that, they were assembled in special camps along with civilian prisoners who had fled to the West from Eastern Europe. In the summer of 1945, they were deported to Moscow. The Red Cross protested in vain. The British writer George Orwell complained that the British press showed no interest in the fate of these men, but he was one of the few public figures who cared about the fate of the Osttruppen.

"Homeric Apologies"

Himmler's initiative to have a large-scale Muslim unit within the framework of the SS came to an inglorious end. It had an arduous history, as the experiences of the experts in the field, Oberländer, Mayer-Mader, Hermann, and Hintersatz, made clear. It was also obvious during the interrogation of a German framework officer, Hugo Heinrich, who was captured by the British in a field hospital in Friedrichsbrunn. Heinrich had been part of the "Neu Turkestan" unit until February 1945. Heinrich incorrectly called Hintersatz Hinterhauer in his statement and told the British about the desertion during Christmas 1944. "The Turkmen did not like to work. The horses we gave them were slaughtered and eaten. They sold their weapons to the partisans. They were busy praying for hours each day. They were extremely sensitive about honorability and easy to offend. German executives were killed for the slightest insult, which happened regularly. They had endless excuses and "Homeric apologies" to avoid heavy work they didn't feel like doing. Everyone looked alike, which allowed them to collect several paychecks. They sympathized with the population they had to control and were almost always indoors. Only two things made the Turkmen ignore the Koran; they loved strong liquor and ate pork as soon as their mullahs were not around."[8]

This outburst symbolized the end of what was once a grand plan. There were opportunities, indeed; Oberländer's theses were in many ways promising. They were certainly more humane and favorable than the racial Nazi occupation policies. Consequently, the alliance between SS and Islam was overthought and did not happen naturally. As became clear, having common enemies does not create a pact in itself. "Neu Turkestan" as a significant military component remained an idea-fixe. The soldiers clinging to their unnatural German partners until the very end had more to do with the soldier's dislike and fear of communism than with sympathy for their German allies.

---

8 Intelligence Summary 12 Corps (British).

The History of the 13. Waffengebirgsdivision der SS "Handschar" (Croat. No. 1)

Aside from the Caucasus Muslims, the Balkans were also a source of recruits for the Reichsführer-SS. It would lead to a series of units, the most important of which would be the "Handschar" division. But working together caused a strange combination of partial pacts and conflicts of interest in these cases as well.

One day, when the battle in Yugoslavia was discussed at the Führer's headquarters in East Prussia, Hitler was informed that the Muslims in the "Handschar" division (named after the Islamic scimitar) were burning down Christian villages rather than fighting Serbian nationalists (Chetniks) and Tito's communist partisans. Some Muslim soldiers allegedly cut out their opponent's heart. Hitler looked up in surprise. "Wurst," he muttered, and the Lagebesprechung continued.

"Wurst" is one of the few statements about the 13. Waffengebirgsdivision der SS "Handschar" by Hitler we know of. This probably exemplifies his lack of interest in the unit, given that Hitler regularly mentioned and discussed many other Waffen-SS volunteer divisions. Therefore, the deployment of Muslims from Bosnia-Herzegovina was mainly concocted by the Reichsführer-SS Heinrich Himmler and the head of the SS Hauptamt-Gottlob Berger. In December 1942, Himmler pleaded with Hitler to establish a purely Muslim unit at the Yugoslavian front lines. Even then, Hitler showed skepticism and believed that the results of other plans should be awaited first. When these military operations did not bring the turbulent Balkan areas under German control, Hitler finally agreed in February 1943. Possibly the disastrous developments around Stalingrad, where the 6th Army went down, played a role in this. The Third Reich could not afford as much racial and ethnic pickiness as they once could. Besides, Himmler believed that the Bosnians were above all of Gothic and Iranian descent and thus not a Slavic people, as he wrote in one of his notes.

But Himmler's interest went deeper than a mere demand for new soldiers. The Waffen-SS, the armed branch of his SS organization, had increasingly become a rival of the regular army. Its role would become even more prominent after the army's debacle in Stalingrad. Since 1943, this "fourth" army branch had been a part of each noteworthy offensive. In addition, Himmler was also fascinated by Islam to

The History of the 13. Waffengebirgsdivision der SS "Handschar"

Division 'Handschar' during the main prayers. The Reichsführer-SS Heinrich Himmler saw good soldiers in the islamic men.

A photo of may 1944. After training in France, the 'Handschar' division functioned reasonably well at first

some extent. Islam, he wrote in one of his letters, taught its followers to be good soldiers who could count on Allah's mercy if they were killed. Also, a German tradition that saw Islam as a natural ally against the British empire influenced Himmler. On many occasions, Kaiser Wilhelm I believed he was the protector of Islam's interests against the British administration. Himmler also believed the 350 million Islamists could be mobilized against the British colonial empire and ungodly communism. From this point of view, it is interesting to note that Berlin's first mosque, established in 1915, was paid for by the German Defense Ministry. The reason may be obvious: Berlin hoped for continued support from Islamic Turkey during World War I. In Himmler's eyes, the Bosnians were the most appropriate link between Arab Islam and National Socialism. The Bosnians were rooted in European history but linked to the Arab world by their faith. This idea drew Himmler to the influential Islamic foreman mentioned earlier, the Grossmufti of Jerusalem, Hadsch Amin el-Hoesseini. El-Hoesseini met with the SS in Berlin on March 24th, 1943, to review plans for a Muslim Waffen-SS unit. He had a brief meeting with Hitler in December 1941. El-Hoesseini admired the Führer and believed that "his anointed hands" would benefit Muslims worldwide. He urged Hitler to appeal to the Islamic world

The History of the 13. Waffengebirgsdivision der SS "Handschar"

The Grossmufti is introduced to the staff of the 13th SS division 'Handschar'

The Grossmufti El-Husseini in conversation with Bosnian volunteers for the Waffen-SS

to start a pro-German, anti-British-Jewish revolt. However, from the perspective of the French (Vichy) mandate territories in North Africa, and because of his future Caucasus plans, Hitler was not yet ready to do so. He deferred the request, saying he would appeal to the Muslims when German forces found their way to Iraq and Iran. El-Hoesseini answered that he had complete confidence in Germany's victory.

Meanwhile, much had happened. There had been major setbacks at the front lines. Advice from Hadsch Amin el-Hoesseini on the recruitment of Muslims for the Waffen-SS was most welcome. This was in part because of the administrative chaos of the Third Reich, above all in the occupied and "friendly" territories. At times, this made it difficult to operate, even for the powerful Reichsführer-SS. A series of obstacles prevented the creation of the "Handschar" division. First, Bosnia-Herzegovina was located within the administrative territory of semi-independent Croatia (NDH), led by Dr. Ante Pavelić. This Croatian nationalist had returned from Italian exile to Zagreb after the German intervention in Yugoslavia. He was pursuing a Greater Croatian idea, which obviously did not leave any room for the more than one million Muslims in Bosnia-Herzegovina. Of the 20 ministerial posts, only two were occupied by Muslims. None of the

Secretaries of State came from the Muslim community. Only thirteen parliamentary representatives were of Muslim origin, while 193 representatives were of Croat-Catholic background.

The second problem was the German Foreign Ministry. Von Ribbentrop was a vain man and had a good relationship with the Pavelić regime. He was not inclined to arm a purely Muslim unit. On top of that, the regular army would compete with Himmler for the few available training grounds in the region and the arming of the unit. Himmler acknowledged he was struggling with the lack of well-trained officers especially and knew he could only call on the army sparsely.

Himmler, however, was also a bureaucratic tiger. He was ruthless where the expansion of his influence was concerned. He chose the best military man in his SS organization, Arthur Phleps. Phleps was a connoisseur of the region and had already established a Balkan division, the 7. SS Freiwillige Gebirgsdivision "Prinz Eugen," which consisted largely of "Volksdeutschen." He put himself at the negotiating table in Zagreb. Given the increasingly problematic military situation, the Croats and Germans quickly agreed it was inevitable to arm more Muslims. Ante Pavelić no doubt remembered his somewhat embarrassing meeting with Hitler at the Werwolf in Winniza in September 1942. At that time, Hitler accused the Croatian authorities of military mismanagement. Despite the mobilization of nearly 150 thousand troops, they had failed to control the mountainous areas of their country without Nazi help. During this discussion, Pavelić successfully blamed the Italians for the military setbacks. But little had changed since then, and Muslim reinforcement had thus become necessary. In the process, Croats in the ranks of the German 100th Jägerdivision on the Don had also suffered heavy losses. However, the idea that more Muslims should be armed was the only conclusion the administration in Zagreb and the SS-Hauptamt agreed on. The primary objection of the Croats was that Himmler and Phleps pursued a purely Muslim unit, partly because of the Arab geopolitical perspective. The Croats, however, were afraid of Bosnian irredentism. They wanted the Muslims under the checkered Croatian flag. Zagreb wanted the unit to become an SS-Ustasa division, with Croatian uniforms and ranks and Croatian as the language of instruction. As a compromise, Zagreb offered 6,000 "volunteers" to help fill the SS-Ustasa division. The SS-Hauptamt saw straight through the intentions of the Croats. This would not create a Muslim division but a mixed division at best. It would give the Croats far too much say in the decision-making process, which Himmler wanted to

Although this photo created 'motorised' impression, the 'Handschar' was a mountain division. There was contantly a lack of officers and good materials

The hunt for the partisans of Tito: Bosnia 1944.

prevent above all. He acted in accordance with Hitler's wishes. Hitler had already made it clear in Winniza to Pavelić that the Croatian army should operate under German supervision.

Himmler chose a delaying tactic. He misled both the Croatian authorities and Von Ribbentrop's ministry, which cherished a good relationship with Zagreb. Phleps and his staff devised a compromise regarding the "Handschar" division. They proposed the unit would consist of an ethnic mix of Volksdeutschen, Catholic Croats, and Muslim Bosnians. Waffen-SS would pay them; they would wear a German uniform and have a Croatian escutcheon on the sleeve. In March 1943, the go-ahead was given for the formation of the divisional staff as a result. It was headed by Herbert von Obwurzer, a Tyrolean officer-gentleman, and the Austrian officer Erich Braun. In the choice of this staff, Himmler's "Habsburg" sentiment seems to have come through somewhat. Himmler did not intend to abide by the agreements with Zagreb and still wanted an all-Muslim division to see the light of day. The plans would simply be ignored, and recruitment of the Muslims would begin. Himmler was prepared to go the extra mile to meet the particular Islamic cultural demands. A SS cookery course was set up in Graz to meet the dietary requirements of the Muslim soldiers. When the Reichsführer-SS visited the divi-

Together with the 'Prinz Eugen'- division in action in the mountains. Over the course of 1944, more and more desertion occured in the 'Handschar' division

sion in Neuhammer in November 1943, he felt that the division's unique headgear, the "Feze," had taken on too much of a Moroccan appearance. He ordered SS-Obergruppenführer Pohl, who was in

Karl-Gustav Sauberzweig, on the right, nicknamed 'de snelle', was the commander of the 'Handschar'-mountain division

charge of the SS-Wirtschaftsverwaltungshauptamt, to repaint and shorten them slightly.

The Reichsführer-SS felt confident about the plans. This is somewhat understandable. Indeed, in

The Grossmufti in conversation with volunteers

the days of the Habsburg Empire, Bosnian units were among the elite troops of the K.U.K. Army. "Those Bosnians" were among the bravest troops. Himmler hoped the new generation of Muslims within the ranks of the Waffen-SS would enter into the same tradition. The SS Hauptamt also rightly believed that many Bosnians were dissatisfied about living as second-class citizens under the Catholic Croatian regime. Gottlob Berger of the SS-Hauptamt informed Himmler that a Christian bishop told him he believed the Bosnian problem would solve itself. A third of them would die in the war, an equal number would flee, and a third would become Christian. Indeed, many in Croatia felt this way. Luckily, throughout the war, humane clergymen were also to be found, as well as in the subse-

Islamic soldiers serving in the Waffen-SS

The Reichsführer-SS Heinrich Himmler wanted to set up two SS-mountaincorpses at the Balkan front. The first corpse was under command of SS-general Phleps, the second corps was to be set up in Hungary, but it never happened

quent communist regime. Cardinal Alojzije Stepina is an example. If anything, the two million Serbs in the Croatian state were even worse off. Many were murdered, deported, or fled to parts of Yugoslavia occupied by the Germans and Italians. With the help of the Grossmufti of Jerusalem, a propaganda offensive was launched in the region. It resulted in 8,000 voluntary enlistments in the "Handschar" division by April 14th, 1943. Much attention was given to the common enemies of Islam and National Socialism: Judaism, Anglo-Americanism, Communism, Freemasonry, and... Catholicism. The result of this propaganda offensive was reasonable but not enough to establish a division. So from then on, the Reichsführer-SS Himmler had to compromise and unintentionally came very close to honoring the (unworkable) agreement made between Phleps and Zagreb. Non-Muslims were now allowed into the ranks of the "Handschar" division, including Volksdeutschen, Catholic Bosnians, and Croats. Additionally, the unit, supplemented by another 2,800 volunteers, became too large for the local training camp in Zemun. The Waffen-SS had to "fight" for training ground and shelter with the army, which was forming the 117th Jäger Division. The result was that the "Handschar" unit could no longer be trained in the region. It had to relocate to Wildflecken, near Le Puy, in France.

Five Bosnian brothers in the 'Handschar' division

The number of problems confronting the new division was now almost incalculable. First, the unit's builders quarreled, Braun and Obwurzen. This was solved by appointing a new commander, Prussian officer Karl-Gustav Sauberzweig. He was the son of a physician and became a war volunteer at the age of 17 in 1914. However, he did not speak any other languages, had only one eye, and was in a persistent state of poor health. Furthermore, there was a chronic shortage of good officers. As many as eleven companies had no commander. There were also hardly any weapons instructors. No one could teach the soldiers of the SS-Geb. Jg. Rgt. 1 and 2, the primary units of "Handschar," how the mortars worked. There was a severe lack of automobiles and

The Grossmufti from Jerusalem inspects the 'Handschar' -division. At El Hoesseini's right is Gustav Sauberzweig, commander of 'Handschar'

horses. Even after completing training, 20 percent of the vehicles were still missing. The kitchen troops did not have enough equipment, so slaughtering livestock was impossible. This created a crazy situation where they had to buy meat from local French butchers. The ethnic diversity of the unit also began to cause problems. Catholic soldiers, in particular, did not feel at home in the unit, which was considered "Muslim" by the SS. The division magazine "Handschar" abundantly covered Bosnia-Herzegovina, but the word "Croatia" was not mentioned anywhere. This discontent about this was understandable. Even in the official German designation of the unit, the word "Croatia" was added behind and in parentheses. The situation led to desertion. The American historian George Lepre mentions a number of 121 Catholic soldiers of "Handschar" deserting in France at the beginning. In contrast, only 13 Muslim soldiers deserted, illustrating that Catholics felt much less at home in "Handschar." Remarkably, four Reichsdeutschen, in addition to 17 Volksdeutschen, also deserted. "They will never become Prussians," one of the German instructors wrote in his diary. Others smirked about them being "Muselgermanen" instead of Muzelmen. The German soldiers maintained their own equipment. New irons were put on their boots each time. The Muselgermans, however, sold the irons directly to the locals and thus wore out their gear in no time. Apparently, the patience of some Germans in the ranks of "Handschar" ran out. They preferred the probably quite difficult desertion in France, from where they tried to escape to Spain.

Things would get even more complicated. Gottlob Berger of the SS-Hauptamt sent out a written warning that Tito had called on his followers to enlist in German service because there were weapons and ammunition to be found there. The Germans were afraid that the ranks of their new allies were infiltrated. Nothing could be further from the truth, however. In fact, the danger was much closer than

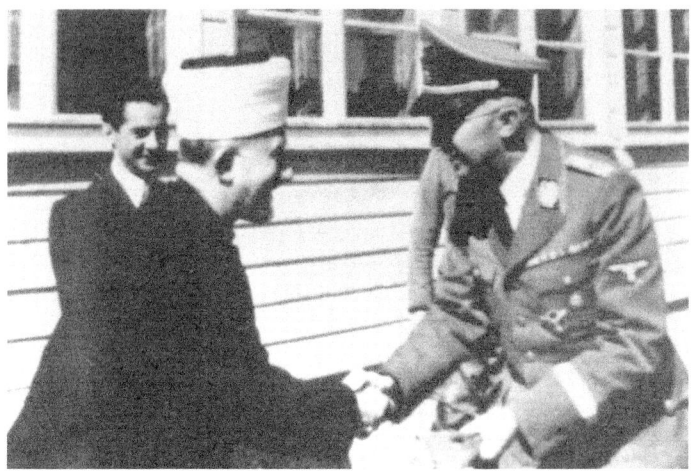

Heinrich Himmler and the Grossmufti

they suspected. In August 1943, several "Handschar" units were posted across various garrisons. The former partisan (!) Ferid Dzanic came into contact with members of the French Resistance, the Maquis, at Hotel Moderne in Villefranche de Rouergue. The presence of other Muslims of Algerian and Moroccan descent in the area made this easier. Dzanic served in the SS-Gebirgs-Pionier-Bataillon 13, making this unit the nucleus of an insurgency. It never became entirely clear why Dzanic chose to revolt and what his future plans were. What is certain, however, is that after the elimination of the German tribal personnel of the pioneer battalion, he wanted to spark, in cooperation with the Maquis, an uprising in the other garrison towns where "Handschar" soldiers stayed. After this, the men possibly wanted to get to the Mediterranean to escape to the Western Allies in North Africa. In any case, it was clear that Dzanic had no shortage of imagination. This plan could not help but end fatally. The first battle, however, was won by the mutineers. The German officers were staying at Hotel Moderne, where everything had been concocted, but they were nonetheless overpowered and, for the most part, executed by the Bosnians. Karl Gustav Sauberzweig reacted furiously as soon as he heard of the uprising. Sauberzweig may have been in poor health, but he was still known as "the fast one." He earned the Iron Cross in World War I by the age of 18. He probably also believed that he did not deserve this. He tried to overcome many difficulties to the best of his abilities and constantly urged his German soldiers to act tactfully. Also, in accordance with Himmler's plans, Sauberzweig paid much attention to the welfare of the Muslims. As a response, non-German soldiers around Villefranche were immediately disarmed. Sauberzweig invaded the town with German troops soon after and ended the uprising. He knew no mercy. Over a dozen mutineers were sentenced to death and executed. At the execution, a strange incident occurred. After the execution of a few "Handschar" soldiers, the name of a soldier who was not among the condemned, but was simply standing in line with the watching pioneer battalion, was suddenly

The History of the 13. Waffengebirgsdivision der SS "Handschar"

German propaganda photo. The caption states that the nazi's and the Islam had a common enemy in the Jews

called up. Sauberzweig asked what he had done. The man had killed his German officer. Sauberzweig had him executed on the spot. The bodies were buried in shallow graves, and over the following days, wild dogs dug up the decomposing bodies. After the war, in 1950, the French and Yugoslav governments placed a small monument honoring the rebellious "Handschar" soldiers.

The German leaders decided that things could not continue like this, although both Hitler and

Gottlob Berger believed the problems had more to do with the presence of the Catholic soldiers. The entire division was moved to the Neuhammer training ground in Germany. Here, Sauberzweig tried to regain control of the unit. They continued the imam training set up by the SS(!) and tried to reverse communist propaganda with counter-propaganda. Especially in the homeland, this had to be done. There were many rumors in Bosnia-Herzegovina. Tito supporters spread the story that the "Handschar" soldiers worked as slaves in the French mines. The people were also hungry and impatiently waiting for the return of the soldiers

Inspection by Heinrich Himmler of the Bosnian Waffen-SS

to the region. It was too early to return, especially given the recent mutiny, but Sauberzweig and Himmler did advocate to support the area with food aid. The soldiers of "Handschar" collected money, and fellow SS divisions gave pay. Grotesque was the generous gesture of the highly controversial SS unit "Dirlewanger." This unit, which would later be the 36. Waffengrenadierdivision der SS, commanded by Dr. Oskar Dirlewanger, gave three months of the division's soldiering. Meanwhile, it committed atrocities on a large scale in Yugoslavia. The gesture of precisely this unit must have had something to do with the deep friendship between the leader of the SS-Hauptamt, Berger, and Dirlewanger, who still knew each other from the Freikorps era.

In October 1943, in Neuhammer, Sauberzweig started aiming for the earliest possible return of "Handschar" to the East in 1944. Meanwhile, important reinforcements followed. A 1,000 new Muslims and hundreds of young German soldiers proved more flexible in this specific situation than the older officers who were replaced. Two closed companies of the 6. SS-Gebirgsdivision "Nord," operating on the Finnish front lines, also arrived at "Handschar." They even briefly considered incorporating captured Indian soldiers (who had been captured on the African front) into "Handschar." But

'Handschar' -soldier of the pioneers divison that was excecuted by Sauberzweig

given the cultural differences, they shied away from this.

In mid-February, it was finally time for "Handschar" to return to its homeland, both regiments now bearing the numbers 27 and 28. They arrived via a long journey, held up by partisan attacks on the rails. Sauberzweig had already reached Phleps' V. SS Mountain Army Corps in Mostar by car, where the local situation was explained to him. A cruel cat-and-mouse game was going on between the occupiers and the partisans. Sauberzweig moved into his headquarters at Hotel Vinkovci. On March 10th of that year, during Operation "Wegweiser," the division was deployed for the first time. The operation ran much like the typical operation on the Yugoslav front. In cluttered mountain terrain, the unit had to clear the Bosut region, as it was used as a supply base. They counted on the presence of about 2,500 communist partisans. The attacking elements were formed entirely by three groups of "Handschar" soldiers: the reconnaissance division (A.A. 13) and regiments 27 and 28. These were divided into small subgroups. At the Save River, Wehrmacht units of the 40th and 42nd Jäger divisions closed off the front, with support given by police units and war boats. The attack was successful. On March 12th, the region was considered safe again.

Osttruppe in prayer

Arrival of the Gross-Mufti at the 'Handschar' division

El Hoesseini's audience with Hitler

No one lived in the town of Bela Crkva at that time. According to a "Handschar" report, the Serbs massacred all the inhabitants. But other German reports only indicated that Serbs were in the region. "Handschar" troops had already been in this town before the unit that wrote the report arrived. During these days, the reports of murdering "Handschar" soldiers came in at the Führer's headquarters. They were forwarded to Hitler by Hermann Fegelein. It seems Hitler did not believe them. He thought that Fegelein had read too many Karl May stories.

As early as April 23rd, "Handschar" was deployed for a new operation, "Maibaum." This time the Heeresgruppe F wanted to cleanse the northeast of Bosnia of partisans. Heeresgruppe F was under the command of Maximilian Freiherr von Weichs, un-

Islamic soldiers serving in the Waffen-SS

'Handschar' -soldiers during actions against Tito-troops

Propaganda material for 'Handschar' soldiers

der which the Yugoslav front fell. A partisan breakthrough into western Serbia, across the Drina River, was feared. In a concentric operation of several units, the area around Sekovici was now to be cleansed. The main units participating in the operation were Rgt. 28 (Raithel) from the Tuzla area, Rgt. 27 (Hampel) from Zvoinik on the banks of the Drina River, and the "Prinz Eugen" division, which advanced towards the north coming from the southern direction, through Han Pijesak to Sekovici. Croatian troops and the SS Fallschirmbataillon 500 supported these units. The operation was a success. In a few days, the area was combed through. It prevented units of the III. Bosnian Corps to penetrate western Serbia. Heeresgruppe F reported nearly a thousand partisan losses and almost a hundred prisoners of war. Despite successes, however, the final goals were not achieved. The area was simply too impassable to cleanse completely. Therefore, on May 17th, Operation "Maiglöckchen" had to be relaunched, a small cleansing operation in which several dozen partisans were killed. After this, things calmed down at the front until June.

Tito was, however, preparing to recapture northeastern Bosnia. In June, as many as three divisions, the 16th and 36th Vojvodina Divisions and the 38th Eastern Bosnian Division, counterattacked. Sauberzweig received word on June 6th that partisans had

'Handschar'-troops readying themselves for action

crossed the Tuzla-Zvoinik road. Not realizing the magnitude of the attack, units of Rgt. 27 and 28 were deployed (Operation "Vollmond") to crush the partisans against the Drina. Battalion I./28, under the command of Heinz Driesner, encountered the full weight of the 16th Vojvodina Division at Priboj, precisely the battalion which had just been replenished with young recruits. They took a hard blow during the heavy fighting that followed and disintegrated. The artillery unit 7/A.R. 13, with four 15-centimeter cannons, was also subdued. The soldiers fired their last salvos point-blank into the lines of partisans. Thirty-eight gunners were killed by the partisans.

Raithel, commander of Rgt. 28, immediately sent the second battalion, I./28, into the battle, as

Artur Phleps in the 'Handschar'-division paper

'Handschar' leaving for battle, may 1944

well as new artillery. Sauberzweig appeared above the battlefield in his Storch aircraft. After a series of chaotic and brutal battles, the Tito attack was finally repelled. "Handschar" suffered 205 losses and 528 wounded. Eighty-nine men were missing. More than 1,500 partisans were killed. The enemy attacks were followed by a series of German anti-partisan actions; "Fliegenfänger," "Heiderose," "Rübezahl," and "Hackfleisch." "Handschar" played an essential role in these operations, together with the "Prinz Eugen" division. All operations led to reasonable results. The first two operations, which they fought near Sekovica, cost Tito almost 1,000 men. A provisional partisan airfield (from which wounded partisans were flown to Italy) was also a

May 1944: battle with Tito-partisans

target. During the last operations, west of Drinjaca, about 250 of Tito's men died.

The continued fighting put considerable pressure on the "Handschar" division, which had never completely overcome its initial problems. In the process, Himmler daydreamed that "Handschar" was only the beginning of his Islamic mountain troops. He now ordered another Islamic Mountain Army Corps to be established, in addition to the V. SS Mountain Army Corps of Phleps, of which "Prinz Eugen" and "Handschar" were a part. The new corps was to consist of Bosnians, Albanians, Croats, and Volksdeutschen, the dangerous combination that had caused "Handschar" so much trouble. New divisions also had to be created. The 23rd

Islamic soldiers serving in the Waffen-SS

Soldiers of the 'Handschar' division during their training in France

Soldiers of the 'Handschar' division take the obstacle course

Waffengebirgsdivision der SS "Kama" (Kama is a dagger) (Croat. No. 2), the 21st Waffengebirgsdivision der SS "Skanderbeg" (Alban. No. 1), and the 24th Waffengebirgskarsjägerdivision der SS would

Commander of the 'Handschar' division, Sauberzweig, at a target practice of his men

together form the IX. SS Mountain Army Corps. Both "Prinz Eugen" and "Handschar" had to give up men and officers to support these new units.

Hot meals for the Bosnian volunteers

This was a major problem, especially for "Handschar." Sauberzweig got involved in the new formation programs and resigned from the division. He was replaced by Desiderius Hampel, who was born a Croat. This underscored, even more, the drift away from the once cherished ethnic composition of "Handschar." Hampel, like Phleps, was one of the eight SS generals who started his military career in the army of the dual monarchy. He was deployed on the front lines for 42 months during World War I. After 1918, Hampel was active primarily in Greater Croatian circles and lived in exile in Vienna and Budapest for extended periods of time. When World War II broke out, he enlisted in the 7th SS Freiwillige Gebirgsdivision "Prinz Eugen" to avoid Hungarian conscription. In Le Puy, he got involved in the "Handschar" division. Regimental Commander Raithel was also among the experienced officers transferred. Raithel became commander of the 23rd Waffengebirgsdivision "Kama." A special storm battalion of 500 Volksdeutschen, the "Einheit Hermann," commanded by Hermann Schifferdecker, was set up to serve as a "Feuerwehr" among the less reliable Islamic units. The new corps was not deployed in the region but in Hungary to avoid Croatian interference.

Meanwhile, the Germans had to fight not only against Tito but also against the Četniks, the nationalist Serbs, who now felt the Germans were slowly starting to lose grip on the region. Things got even worse due to the relentless acts of sabotage, sting operations, and major offensives by the partisans, the approaching Eastern Front, and the elimination of Italy as an ally - which in turn created tension between Zagreb and Berlin about the management of the Dalmatian coast. A Sonderbevollmächtigten Südost was appointed urgently, Hermann Neubacher. Now that it was clear that Tito was the most significant power factor, Neubacher was to ensure that all anti-Communist forces in the region were brought together. This led to challenging cooperation between Berlin, Zagreb and the Četniks of Serbia (D. Mihajlovic), and Montenegro under Pavle Djurisic. Djurisic had

The History of the 13. Waffengebirgsdivision der SS "Handschar"

'Handschar', may 1944

been a German prisoner of war in Poland, where he escaped. He was now armed and deployed by the Germans against the Communists. Neubacher pointed out that he could not guarantee the

Montenegrins would limit their armed actions to Tito.

In August 1944, Croatian General Franjo Simic was assassinated by Četniks in Mostar, leading to atrocities back and forth. The Croats called the Serbs "treacherous snakes," "Četniks communists," and "Byzantine thugs" and called for revenge. Even when the Četniks were forced to fall back westward after the fall of Belgrade, Croatian revenants stood by and committed carnage. Neubacher sent a letter to Berlin to alarm them; surely one could not let German allies slaughter other German allies!

In addition to summary judgment executions, thousands languished in Croatian concentration camps. Jasenovac was the most notorious. Although relatively unknown in the West, these camp histories remain scars in the region's past. Split's German city commander now threatened to execute five Ustasas for every Četnik murdered. "Only terror seems to help now," German officer Glaise-Horstenhaus telegraphed to his authorities. To further complicate the people mix, German-minded Cossacks of the Pannwitz Corps were also deployed in the region. The Heeresgruppe F reported that "the Cossacks indulge in alcohol, pillage, and rape so much, and have so little respect for life - including their own - that it is only paralleled in the Thirty

Years' War." As "Panslavists," the Cossacks in the "German civil war" within the Yugoslav war would especially direct their hatred against the Catholic Croats. As a result of this general picture of disintegration, no less than 2,000 soldiers of "Handschar" deserted in September. The "Kama" division also suffered desertions. In October, the month in which the Tito Partisans and the Soviets liberated Belgrade, 700 "Handschar" soldiers had already served in the ranks of the III. Bosnian Partisan Corps, according to the historian Lepre.

Reichsführer-SS Himmler immediately called on Sauberzweig and made his disappointment clear in harsh terms. These disastrous developments did not match Himmler's grand-Islamic aspirations. A series of new plans were vetted. They could "renounce" the "Bosniaks" and transfer the units to the Croatian army, but Himmler did not want to give up just yet. He once again mobilized the Grossmufti and a whole flock of imams to join the new army corps in Budapest and Yugoslavia to support the Muslim troops. Also, at Sauberzweig's urgent request, Himmler wanted to significantly increase the division's German staff. It was to include 3,000 German soldiers from the island of Crete. While these plans were in full swing, the fighting continued. The construction of the new army corps in Hungary suffered because of increasing Soviet pressure on the Theiss front. In Yugoslavia, the fighting in Janja and Vukosavci continued, and another 600 "Handschar" soldiers fled.

Patience ran out. Himmler demanded of Sauberzweig that there be no more desertions. In the background, things were collapsing. After the fall of Romania (in August), Bulgaria (in September), and the liberation of Eastern Yugoslavia (in October), the Germans were in the middle of retreating from Greece, where Heeresgruppe E (Löhr) resided. They had to fight their way through the partisan territory, through Sarajevo to the west. Meanwhile, they had to hold off the Red Army on the eastern flank. All that remained for Himmler was to disarm unreliable Bosnian soldiers. In Operation "Herbstlaub," army units were deployed, the 1st Gebirgsdivision and the 118th Infantry Division, to disarm more than 3,000 "Handschar"

Artur Phleps, Himmlers trustee at the Balkan. He negotiated with the Kroatian authorities

soldiers. The "Kama" division was disbanded entirely. These drastic measures meant that the "Handschar" division consisted of as many German soldiers as Bosnian soldiers by November.

It was precisely this new - more reliable - composition that caused "Handschar" to return to frontline deployment quickly after all. Romania was no longer present in front of the Axis. Starting in late December 1944, heavy fighting occurred near Budapest. The staff of the IX. SS Mountain Army

Bosnian woman with a volunteer of the 'Handschar' -division

Corps, under the command of Karl von Pfeffer-Wildenbruch, was deployed to defend the Hungarian capital, although it had no mountain troops but cavalry divisions ("Florian Geyer" and "Maria Theresia"). They persevered against the Red Army until February 13th, 1945. Disengagement attempts in January (the "Konrad" operations) and the great March offensive "Frühlingserwachen" could not free the surrounded city. "Handschar" was deployed as part of Heeresgruppe Süd (commanded by Otto Wöhler and later Lothar Rendulic) on the front lines south of Lake Balaton, which ran to the Drau (Drava). By the time the "division Handschar" arrived, the Germans were greatly distressed. The soviets were forming bridgeheads by the Drava and threatening to advance into the hinterland of the 2nd Pz. Army (which was guarding the region south of Lake Balaton for Heeresgruppe Süd - including the oil fields at Nagykanisza, which were vital to Hitler). A quickly formed combat group, the SS Kampfgruppe Hanke, commanded by SS-Sturmbannführer Hanke, was transported to Hercegszöllös and deployed there. In the process, the three battalions and a small artillery division suffered the heaviest losses since the creation of "Handschar." Lepre assumes that the Red Army killed about 1,000 of the 1,200 men of the Kampfgruppe. On November 26th, the unit was rushed away from the front and assigned to the 44th

Wounded are transported after battle with Tito's troops

Hoch-und-Deutschmeister infantry division, an Austrian unit.

Himmler again considered removing the "Handschar" division and re-establishing it at a troop training site in Poland. But increasing pressure on the Hungarian front prevented him from making this decision. "Handschar" was stationed on the east side of the Nagykanizsa oil fields in the so-called Dorethea-Stellung, which connected to the Margarethestellung between Lake Velence and Lake Balaton and ran up to the Drava. "Handschar" stood between alternating units here. Among them was the H.u.D. Division, the 71st Infantry Division, and the 16th SS Panzergrenadierdivision "Reichsführer-SS," commanded by SS-Oberführer Baum, which had been brought in from the Italian front. In January and early February, during operations "Konrad" north of Lake Balaton, "Handschar" remained relatively quiet. But fighting resumed in the area of the 2nd Pz. Army after the Soviets repelled Operation "Konrad-III," the third liberation attempt of Budapest by the IV. SS-Pz. Corps [Gille], in late January and captured Budapest after 52 days of siege. "Handschar" was still a weak division, despite small additions, including several dozen fanatical Hungarian Arrow Cross fascists. These fascists were supporters of the Hungarian pro-German politician Ferenc Szálasi, who had replaced Admiral Horthy after negotiation attempts with the Allies. They were good soldiers, but most died soon. In March 1945, operation "Frühlingserwachen" began north of Lake Balaton, the last major German of-

Bosnian Waffen-SS in conversation with locals

fensive on the Eastern Front. The 6th SS Pz. Army, commanded by Sepp Dietrich, attacked the Soviet positions on the west bank of the Danube, together with the army brought in from the Ardennes, but without success. Ten days later, the Red Army's Vienna operation began, upon which the elite units of the Waffen-SS retreated to Austria. Obviously, if Himmler's elite units could not persevere, "Handschar's" situation did not look rosy either. In late March, Russian and Bulgarian units attacked the front of the 2nd Pz. Army. The front at Nagykanizsa was forced to withdraw. In early April, the oil fields fell into Russian hands. "Handschar," together with other army units, crossed the Mura River and retreated to the Reichsschutzstellung on the

Mountain artillery of 'Handschar' in action, may 1944

Austro-Hungarian border. After this, they made a remarkable decision. The division's imams stated that many Bosnians wanted to return to their homeland. With the war rapidly rushing westward, they did not feel very inclined to continue fighting. Hans Hanke discussed the situation with Hampel, the division commander who had his headquarters at All Saints. They decided to let the soldiers go who did not want to continue. This basically ended Himmler's dream of a Bosniak SS division. Many preferred the uncertain journey home, even though hundreds did not survive it. The remnants of the division fell into Western Allied captivity shortly after that. The first division commander of "Handschar," Sauberzweig, also found himself in British captivity. He committed suicide in 1946 when he learned the Western Allies wanted to extradite him to Yugoslavia.

Looking back on the "Handschar" experiment, it is clear that Himmler's Grand Islamist plans were far too ambitious. The same can be said about the geopolitical benefits he thought he could derive from them. The plans lacked support within its own ranks, the German Foreign Ministry. There was inadequate weapon capacity and a lack of instructors and officers. Furthermore, there was a constant conflict with the Croats about competence. This got so out of hand that Himmler sometimes forbade using "Handschar" to bring in the Croatian harvest because, "after all, the Croats were so eager to be 'independent.'" Different opinions were also heard within the SS. Some believed the Bosnians could never become "Prussians." Others did their best, such as Sauberzweig. But they were mainly "nur-Soldaten," lacking proper training for such complicated experiments. Also, Himmler was impatient. First, he undermined "Prinz Eugen" in favor of "Handschar" and later "Handschar" in favor of "Kama" and the other experiments. On top of that, the Germans failed to win over a broad stratum of Bosnians, despite the Habsburg sentiments in the region and despite the help of the Grossmufti and other spiritual leaders. Himmler himself attached great importance to his Muslim army. That much is evident. He tried to construct a real army of them until the very end, and not entirely without results. Parts of the division functioned reasonably well. But strenuous relationships and a lack of men and materials prevented optimal deployment.

Nevertheless, on April 16th, 1944, Gottlob Berger complimented Sauberzweig on the deployment of the "Handschar" division and its role in stabilizing the situation in Bosnia. The last commander, ss-Brigadeführer (since January 1945) Hampel, even obtained the Ritterkreuz in May 1945. But the marriage of scimitar and swastika remained difficult to the end, despite all their common enemies. Yugoslavia was left ransacked, with 1.2 million dead, most of them murdered by fellow countrymen. The Grand Croatian leader Pavelić promptly defected to Argentina. He died in Madrid in 1959.

"Skanderbeg" - the Albanian SS

The history of the 21. Waffengebirgsdivision der SS "Skanderbeg" is even more unknown than the history of the "Handschar" division. "Skanderbeg" was composed of Albanian Muslims, mainly from the current Kosovo region. In many ways, it resembled "Handschar." The Germans had difficulty empathizing with the Islamic character of the unit, and there was also a lack of German managerial personnel. Because of this, Foreign Affairs made a call via Martin Luther to win over an additional 10,000 Volksdeutschen to the German cause. This was supposed to give the units some backbone.

Albanian-German cooperation proved to be complicated. They had an aversion to the old Yugoslav regime in common, a regime that was authoritarian and centralist and left the Albanians little autonomous space. For this reason, the local army group F commander, General August Winter, emphasized the opportunities to win over the Albanians for the German cause. He followed the vision of Albania expert Franz von Scheiger, who pointed this out as early as 1941. SS officers such as the

Recrutment of volunteers for the 'Skanderbeg' division

HSSPF SS-Gruppenführer, August Meyszner, and the special delegate for the SS in Albania, Josef Fitzthum, followed his lead.

Two affiliated organizations could help the Germans in this regard, the Second League of Prizren and the Committee for the Defense of Kosovo. Both of these organizations were not so much pro-fascism but did aim at controlling Serbian and Montenegrin influence in the border region of Albania and former Yugoslavia. The three most prominent frontmen within this movement were Bedri Pejani, publisher of the newspaper *Populli*, Xhaver Deva, an Albanian intellectual who had studied in Vienna and Istanbul, and Rexhep Mitrovica, who was originally a teacher and very involved in the Greater Albanian cause.

Problems arose, however, when the Germans were unwilling to pay the ultimate price to win the Albanians to their cause. The Albanians wanted their "own army," but that was too big of an ask for the Germans. In exchange for this, the Albanian leaders agreed to provide 100,000 troops. But when the Germans failed to keep their promises, the Albanians and Kosovars did not even deliver the first 10,000 men. A complex game of chess began. It did not help that the Italians were also still an occupying force in the region and had their own agenda. As a result, complicated partial pacts that did not last were a fact of life. League militias were primarily concerned with driving Montenegrins and Serbs out of the Greater Albany areas. Hermann Neubacher, the Sonderbeauftragter Südost, was so astounded by this that he depicted Pejani, one of the driving forces behind this policy, as a lunatic in one of his reports. The Albanians, while praised for their wariness by the Germans, were also difficult to control. Pejani moved around the country with his private militia, up to a thousand men strong. According to German documents, a small army of "half-savages" came along when he came to Tirana for meetings.

Nevertheless, efforts were made to create the division near Prizren. The unit came under the command of SS-Brigadeführer August Schmidhuber. It

The Albanians were the last possible source of volunteers the SS could use. In the photo: Wehrmacht-soldiers surrounded by ethnic Albanians

was also temporarily led by the division's Ib, SS-Obersturmbannführer Alfred Graf, after Schmidhuber was struck with yellow fever. The division's strength got stuck at barely 4,000 men, and attempts were made to find reinforcements elsewhere. The so-called Albanian battalion of "Handschar" was transferred to the sister division "Skanderbeg." The men protested. They had a particularly close relationship with the commander of "Handschar," Sauberzweig. Nevertheless, on May 7th, 1944, the troops arrived in Prizren. They also tried to recruit the Albanians who were still prisoners of war. The non-compliance of real life became apparent in this case too. It can no longer be estab-

German high staff and Albanian volunteers pass by a tank of Italian origin, Yugoslavia end 1944

lished how many Albanians were released exactly, it was somewhere between 10,000 and 20,000 men, but it is certain that only a fraction of those men arrived at "Skanderbeg" to report for duty.

To give the unit more backbone, Volksdeutsche volunteers from other units, such as "Prinz Eugen" and "Handschar," were also added. Otto Kumm, who led "Prinz Eugen" since January 30th, 1944, provided Volksdeutschen from the SS-Freiw.Geb. Jg.Rgt.13 for this purpose. They even brought in navy personnel from occupied Greece. Their contribution turned out to be quite memorable; they wrote the melancholic Skanderbeg song.

Albanian volunteers for the 'Skanderbeg' division

The military side of things remained tricky for "Skanderbeg." Schmidhuber reported that the Albanians performed well during Operation "Draufgänger" in July 1944. Still, it did become clear to the volunteers that they had bet on the wrong horse. One of the League's conditions for supporting the Germans was believing in their final victory. That image was falling apart. Also, the fact that the German leaders were not Muslim created a certain distance between the officers and the men. Things became even more unstable when Fitzthum and other SS officers tried to bolster their positions by bringing in paramilitary units that fell under the command of the various clan heads. This fragmented the German forces even further. At best, these were partial pacts of a temporary nature. The clan militias were anti-communist above all and shared very few other interests with the German occupiers. In some instances, the Germans issued ammunition to these national militias, only to be used against them shortly after. The Germans required the paramilitary units to turn in up to 70% of the bullet casings after military actions to be sure they were fighting, not collecting weapons against them. On top of that, there were many shortages anyway, especially regarding communication equipment, but even the uniforms were a problem. Unlike in "Handschar," the Fez, the characteristic headgear mentioned earlier, did not serve in "Skanderbeg." For the Albanians, it was too much of an Ottoman symbol, incompatible with the Albanians' desire for autonomy.

From a military perspective, "Skanderbeg" concentrated on keeping the roads in the Kosovo area safe, and it participated in Nazi partisan operations, such as Operation "Junikäfer," "Falkenauge," "Fuchsjagd," "Rübezahl," and the like. "Junikäfer" was the first operation, which began on June 26th, 1944. The threatened area around the chromite ore production near Kepenik was at stake. It was threatened by the partisans of the Gani Beg group. The soldiers from "Handschar" were mainly deployed for this, and the deployment was reasonably successful. The partisans were fended off. Schmidhuber did note, however, that the partisans returned, reinforced, soon after. "Falkenauge" was a cleansing operation from Struga to Elbasan. On July 10th and 11th, this involved heavier fighting with partisans. They were supported by German army units, divisions 181 and 297, who helped ensure that "Skanderbeg" stood its ground. On July 11th, however, the operation ran into heavy resistance and came to an end. "Draufgänger" followed between July 18th and 28th, 1944, around Berane. Here "Skanderbeg" faced its first major setbacks. The Tito partisans overran a non-commissioned officer unit of 150 men, despite support from the First German Mountain Division and "Prinz Eugen." The partisans were simply much stronger and caused the deployed units of "Skanderbeg" great trouble. Franziska A. Zaugg researched the history of "Skanderbeg" and concluded that during the summer of 1944, the balance of forces absolutely shifted in favor of the partisans. In subsequent operations, the goal was no longer to surround and destroy the partisans. There was no longer strength for that. All they wanted now was to disassemble them and keep them away from their supply bases.

In addition to these military actions, Albanian Muslims were also involved in setting up and guarding the concentration camp "Pristina." The history

Waffen-Gebirgs-Division der SS 'Skanderbeg'

of this camp was described only sporadically. In any case, it is clear that units of the Albanian troops of the "Handschar" division transferred to "Skanderbeg" were involved in this camp. Also, "Skanderbeg" was a part of the units that hunted Jews and Communists and arrested several hundred of them. A document dated mid-July 1944 speaks of 600 prisoners in the camp. SS-Sturmbannführer Bauer was in charge of Pristina. In general, by the way, few Jews lived in this region.

When the tables turned in the war, the number of desertions increased. Near Tetovo, nearly 1,000 men of the Waffen-geb.Jäg.Rgt SS 50 deserted.

German troops were also increasingly attacked. The Germans initially struck back with public executions, but eventually, they became too weak even to do that. The "Skanderbeg" unit was known for retaliating until late in the war. The hanging of some female partisans caused great turmoil among the population. By October 1944, the unit was weakened so much that it was taken apart, scaled down to regimental strength, and divided into several combat groups. The entire regiment was commanded by 86 German officers, 467 non-commissioned officers (including 38 Albanians), and still had 887 teams, of which 499 were Albanian, aside from 3504 Albanian recruits. After the heavy losses in the battle for the Cakor Pass, hardly any Albanians remained. The Kampfgruppe, now commanded by Alfred Graf, was reinforced with (German) police units and navy personnel from Greece. "Skanderbeg" retreated westward, together with the German infantry divisions 181 and 297, starting in October 1944. On November 8th, the goal was Sarajevo. The artillery division was lost in a Bulgarian aerial bombardment. On December 4th, the division arrived in Vlasenica at a former Tito base. Parts of the division merged into the "Prinz Eugen" unit and moved on with them. Others went their own way. Near Begovopolje, they were attacked by partisans, but "Skanderbeg" managed to repel this attack. On

December 22nd, 1944, "Skanderbeg" was ordered to set up camp at Bijeljina and turn this area into a fortress. Both Russian and Bulgarian troops and Tito partisans were facing them. It seemed like this would become the last bastion for "Skanderbeg," but on the 23rd, German army units came to relieve them. The site was abandoned on the 28th. Not much is known about what happened in the following weeks. At Kopf Sl.Brod, remnants of the division were absorbed into "Prinz Eugen." Navy personnel was taken from the division and moved to Ostfriesland. From then on, they wore the bracelet "Skanderbeg." Other parts of the division, such as the SS-Wirtschafts-Btl. 21, still made it all the way to the Oder, where it went down fighting the Red Army.

Resources

Annaorazov, J., *Turkmenistan during the Second World War.* In: *Journal of Slavic Military Studies* (2012).

Aus dem Leben des Hadsch Amin el- Husseini. Die Rolle des Grossmufti. In: *Die Zeit,* no.40 (September 28th 1990).

Ausschuss für Deutsche Einheit (hg.), *Die Wahrheit über Oberländer.*

Bailey, R.H., *Partisans and Querrillas* (1978).

Blood, P.W., *Hitler's Bandit Hunters. The SS and the Nazi Occupation of Europe* (Washington, 2008).

Bogaard, G., *Jasenovac, sterfhuis voor levende doden.* In: *Reformatorisch Dagblad,* (April 30th 1998).

Böhler, J./Gerwarth, R. (ed.), *The WAFFEN-SS. A European History.*

Braunbuch über die verbrecherische faschistische Vergangenheit des Bonner Ministers (Berlin, 1960).

Bulajic, M., *"Jasenovac Myth" Genocide against the Serbs, Jews and Gypsies* (Belgrade, 1994).

Christensen, C.B./Scharff Smith,P./Poulsen,N.B., *De Waffen-SS. Het Europese leger van de Nazi's* (Rotterdam, 2016).

Davies, N., *Warschau 1944. De gedoemde opstand van de Polen* (Utrecht, 2004).

Dear, I.C.B./Foot, M.R.D., *The Oxford Companion of the Second World War* (Oxford/New York, 1995).

Dedijer, V., *Jasenovac-das jugoslawische Auschwitz und der Vatikan* (Freiburg, 1991).

Donlagic, A./Atanckovic, Z./Plenca, D., *Yugoslavia in the Second World War* (Belgrade, 1967).

Dossena, P.A., *Hitler's Turkestan Soldiers. A History of the 162nd (Turkistan) Infantry Division* (Solihull, 2015).

Gosztony, P., *Endkampf an der Donau 1944/45* (Wien/München/Zürich, 1969).

Gosztony, P., *Hitler's Fremde Heere. Das Schicksal der nichtdeutschen Armeen im Ostfeldzug* (Düsseldorf/Wien, 1976).

Heff, J., *Nazi Germany and the Arab and Muslim World: Old and New Scholarship* (2008).

Heiber, H., *Hitler's Lagebesprechungen. Die Protokollfragmente seiner militärischen Konferenzen 1942-1945* (Stuttgart, 1962).

Hillgruber, A. (Hg), *Staatsmänner und Diplomaten bei Hitler. Vertrauliche Aufzeichnungen über Unterredungen mit Vertretern des Auslandes 1939-1941* (Frankfurt am Main, 1967).

Hoffmann, J., *Die Ostlegionen 1941-1943* (Freiburg, 1981).

Hoffmann, J., *Deutsche und Kalmyken 1942-1945* (Freiburg, 1986).

Hoffmann, *Caucasia 1942/43. Das deutsche Heer und die Orientvölker der Sowjetunion* (Freiburg, 1991).

Höpp, G., *Was Muslime in Deutschland oft nicht wissen.* In: *Frankfurter Allgemeine Zeitung* (June 2nd 1993).

Hory, L/Broszat, M., *Der kroatische Ustascha-Staat 1941-1945.* In: *Schriftenreihe der vierteljahrshefte für Zeitgeschichte* (1965).

Jeloschek, A./Richter, F./Schütte, E./Semler, J., *Freiwillige vom Caucasus. Georgier, Armenier, Aserbaidschaner, Tschetschenen u.a. auf deutscher Seite. Der "Sonderverband Bergmann" und sein Gründer Theodor Oberländer* (Graz/Stuttgart, 2003).

Kalben, H- D., Zur Geschichte des XV.Kosaken-Kavallerie Korps (Deutsches Soldaten Jahrbuch 1963).

Krannhals, H. von, Der Warschauer Aufstand 1944.

Krätschmer, E.G., Ritterkreuzträger der WAFFEN-SS.

Lepre, G., Himmler's Bosnian Division. The WAFFEN-SS Handschar Division 1943- 1945 (1997).

Mallmann, K-M./Paul, G. (hg.), Karrieren der Gewalt. Nationalsozialistische Täterbiographien.

Meulenkamp, W., Eastern Approaches, de oorlog van Fitzroy Maclean. In: Pierik/Ros (ed.), Tweede Bulletin van de Tweede Wereldoorlog (Soesterberg 2000).

Mitcham, S.W., Hitler Legions. German Army Order of Battle World War II (1984).

Motadel, D., Islam and Nazi Germany's War (2014).

Münchhausen, K. von, Der Traum vom grossen Arabien. In: Die Zeit, no.37 (August 1990).

Nicosia, F.R., Nazi Germany and the Arab World (Cambridge, 2015).

Pfeiffer, R., Der Osttürkische Waffen-Verband der SS (Internet).

Pierik,P., Hungary 1944-45, The Forgotten Tragedy (Soesterberg, 1995).

Preradovisch, N. von, Die Generale der WAFFEN-SS (Berg am See, 1985).

Rauchensteiner, M., Der Krieg in Österreich 1945 (Wien, 1984).

Rullmann, H.P., Tito. *Vom Partisan zum Staatsmann* (Munich, 1980).

Scheurig, B., *Volksaufstand gegen das Hitlerregime. Die Tragödie des slowakischen Freiheitskampfes 1944* (Article, 1971).

Schachinger, W., *Die Bosniaken kommen! Elitetruppe in der k.u.k. Armee 1879- 1919* [1989] (Wien, 1994).

Stein, G.H., *Geschichte der W<small>AFFEN</small>-SS* (Düsseldorf, 1978).

Telpuchowski, B.S., *Die Sowjetische Geschichte des Grossen Vaterländischen Krieges 1941- 1945* (Frankfurt am Main, 1961).

Tessin, G., *Verbände und Truppen der deutschen Wehrmacht und Waffen SS im Zweiten Weltkrieg 1939-1945*, Sechster Band (Osnabrück, 1972).

Tieke, W./Rebstock, F., *Im letzten Aufgebot. Die 18. SS-Freiwilligen-Panzergrenadier-Division Horst Wessel* (Coburg, 1995).

Tolstoy, N., *Die Verratenen von Yalta* (Munich, 1985).

Venohr, W., *Aufstand der Slowaken. Der Freiheitskampf von 1944* (Berlin, 1992).

Vermaat, E., *Hitler en de Arabieren* (Soesterberg, 2016).

Voigt, H., *Die "verlorene Haufen", Sondertruppen zur Frontbewährung im 2.Weltkrieg. Ein Beitrag zu ihrer Geschichte-Teil IV*. In: *Deutsches Soldaten Jahrbuch 1986.*

Wachs, P-C., *Der Fall Theodor Oberländer (1905-1998). Ein Lehrstück deutscher Geschichte* (Frankfurt am Main, 2000).

Wiesenthal, S., *Grossmufti, Grossagent der Achse* (Wien, 1947).

Zaugg, F.A., *Albanische Muslime in der W<small>AFFEN</small>-SS. Von "Grossalbanien" zur Division "Skanderbeg"* (2016).

Zeitgeschichtlichen Forschungsstatt Ingolstadt (hg.), Theodor Oberländer, *Der Osten und die Deutsche Wehrmacht. Sechs Denkschriften aus den Jahren 1941-43 gegen die NS Kolonialthese* (Asendorf, 1987).

Zewell, R., *Die Nation hat ihren Märtyrer.* In: *Merkur Plus,* No. 41 (Oct. 9, 1998).

Internet/archives

http://www.lexikon-der-wehrmacht.de/Gliederungen/SichDiv/444SichDiv.htm

www.warsawuprising.com/paper/rona.htm

GDIR (German Docs in Russia)

Archives Vopersal

National Archives Washington

Bundesarchiv Koblenz